TRIAL

Paperback edition first published in the UK in 2007 by University of Plymouth Press, Scott Building, Drake Circus, Plymouth, Devon, PL4 8AA, United Kingdom.

A catalogue record of this book is available from the British Library

ISBN 978-1-84102-170-6

Library of Congress Cataloging in Publication

Editor: Andrew Brown

Book design: Brian Guerin, Tsz Hang Tsang, Anna Kolesnik

TRIAL

A study of the devising
process in Reckless Sleepers'
'Schrödinger's Box'

by

Andrew Brown

Mole Wetherell

& Reckless Sleepers

This book is comprised of four different voices:

the black text was written by Andrew Brown,

the green cursive text was written by Mole Wetherell.

the red text was written by Reckless Sleepers or describes processes used by the company

and the blue text provides the performance text and directions from
'Schrodinger's Box', as performed in 1998

Thanks to: Tim Ingram, Leen Dewilde, Ine Naessens, Tom Roden, Dan Belasco Rogers, Jake Oldershaw, Sarah Dawson, Marie Fitzpatrick, Sara Richards, Rosie Garton, Becky Lodge, Lucia Hogg, Andy Clarke, Barbara Raes, Colin Brown, Tim Brown, Teresa Niedojadlo, John Newling, Pete Bowcott, Terry Shave, Judith Mottram, Rocket Scenery

Photographs: Dario Rumbo, Mole Wetherell, Simon Howell, Andrew Brown, Reckless Sleepers

Andrew Brown's own artistic practices centre upon processes involving text, and the relationship between sound and moving image. He is co-founder of the independent press Tak Tak Tak, and music/film ensemble Left Hand Right Hand. His interest in the work of Reckless Sleepers was triggered by witnessing 'Parasite' in 1993. He has written extensively about contemporary performance over the past decade.

Mole Wetherell has been making theatre projects for Reckless Sleepers since he initiated the project in 1988. He works as an artist in the visual arts and theatre.

A DVD document of performances of 'Schrödinger's Box' has been made to accompany this book and is available from www.reckless-sleepers.co.uk

CONTENTS

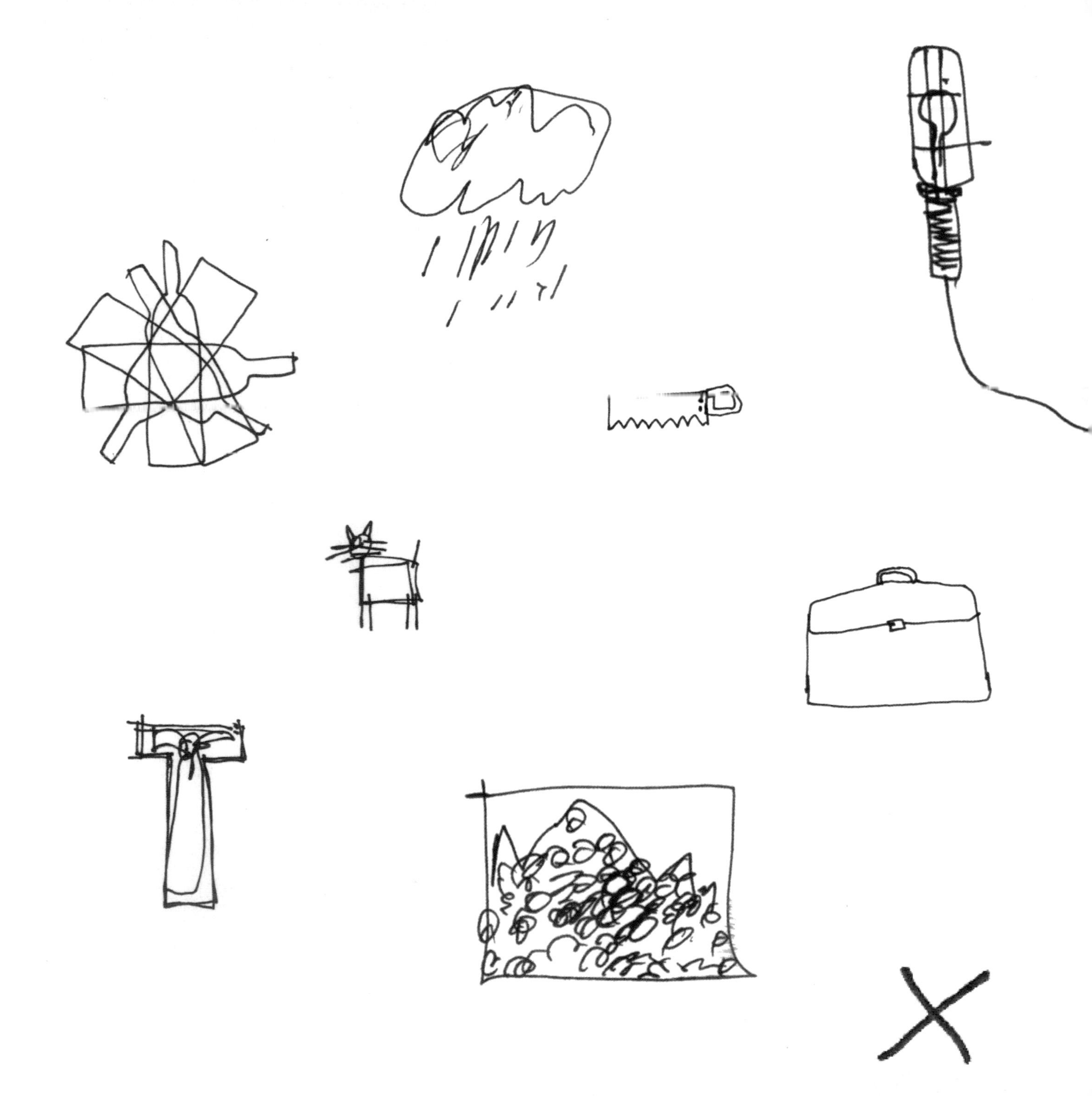

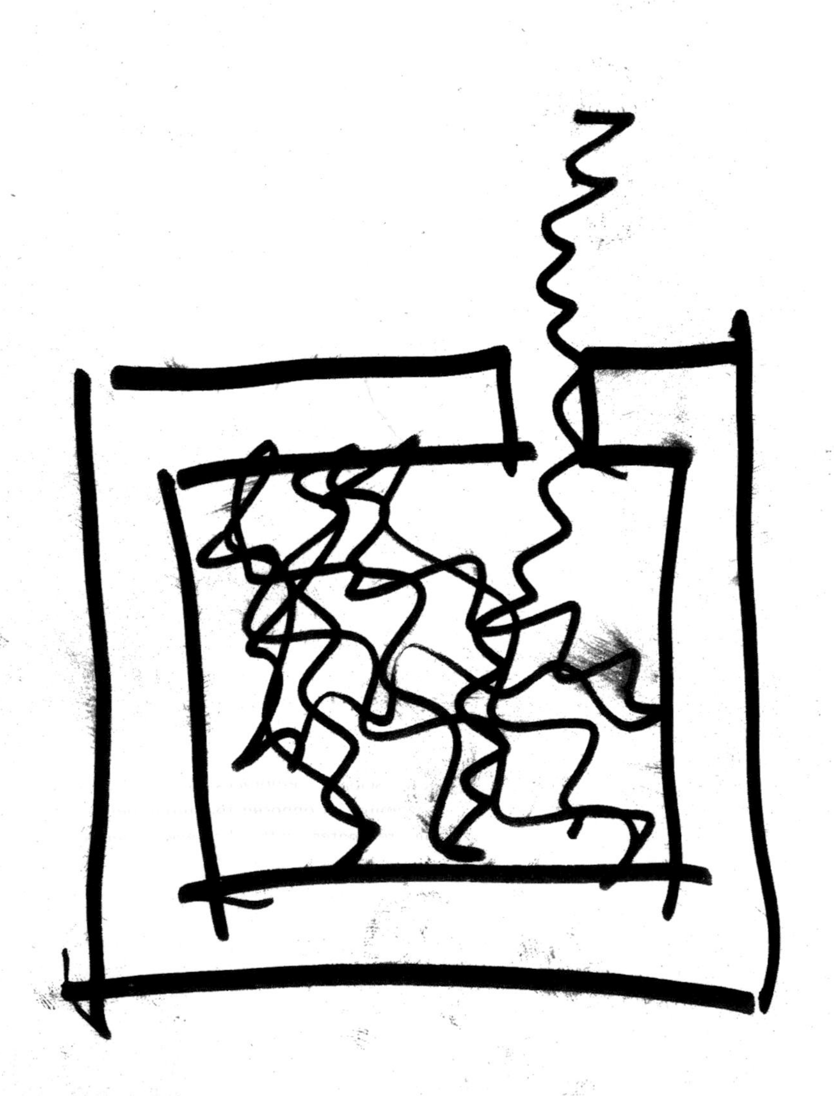

'Trial' is about the process of art, the engagement with and representation of personal thoughts and beliefs, collective myth, the work of other artists, scientists and thinkers. It takes as a case study the output of Reckless Sleepers, a creative company that makes innovative and experimental visual art and performance, and in particular its collectively devised performance 'Schrödinger's Box' (1997).

Intoduction

PROCESS

'Trial' is an attempt to explore and express the processes that Reckless Sleepers uses in the devising of material. It also seeks to make connections with underlying principles and concepts. 'Trial' is concerned with ideas and the role of collaboration in their development. It is an elucidation, demystification and celebration of Reckless Sleepers and the diversity of its work.

This book has itself come about through a collaboration involving freelance writer Andrew Brown, Reckless Sleepers' Creative Director Mole Wetherell and other artists who work with the company. This activity has been supported in part by 'A-Trophy', a three-year research project proposed by the company and funded by The Arts Council of England, by which the initial phases of various new company projects have been supported. A key aspect has been the re-devising in 2006 of 'Schrödinger's Box' in Gent. This has provided research opportunities beyond trawling through archives and retrospective interviews, into a direct encounter with the devising process. When considered alongside original documentation the effects of the passing of time, changes in location, personnel and wider circumstances become apparent. The re-devising has opened up 'Schrödinger's Box' and revealed much that can be developed further, demonstrating the benefits of allowing time for material to mature and minds to reflect.

New science embraces the notion of 'becoming' as opposed to simply 'being' and this resonates with the acknowledgment of the significance of process. Performance is exemplary among art forms for its characteristic of non-fixity. All are in a state of becoming, neither whom we were nor will become.

In Marshall and Zohar's (1997, p.183) articulation of Heisenberg's 'Uncertainty Principle' they assert that 'we can never be both detached observers and involved participants' and the authors of 'Trial' proudly acknowledge themselves as the latter. The notion of the objective observer is itself problematic and such critique will be left for others to perform. In the meantime full use of partiality will be made in opening up Reckless Sleepers' hitherto unseen processes.

This might seem to be a strategy of some risk, as the effectiveness of live performance is often dependent upon partial and gradual revelation. A further risk, in emphasising process over finished product might be to give a misleading impression of a lack of rigour. In fact rigour, the conscious calculation that can be understood to work in dynamic opposition with intuitive insight (Bannerman, 2004), is evident in both workshop and stage performance. Although witnessing a workshop onstage might prove a step too far, some of its mechanics may prove worthy of study. A knowing reader with their inquisitiveness engaged may find greater meaning and pleasure in the work.

Whilst this book is not intended as a guide to 'making theatre', it explores models that have proven useful for Reckless Sleepers. The relationship with the company's concerns and aesthetic has been explored, hopefully providing material for further discussion and adaptation.

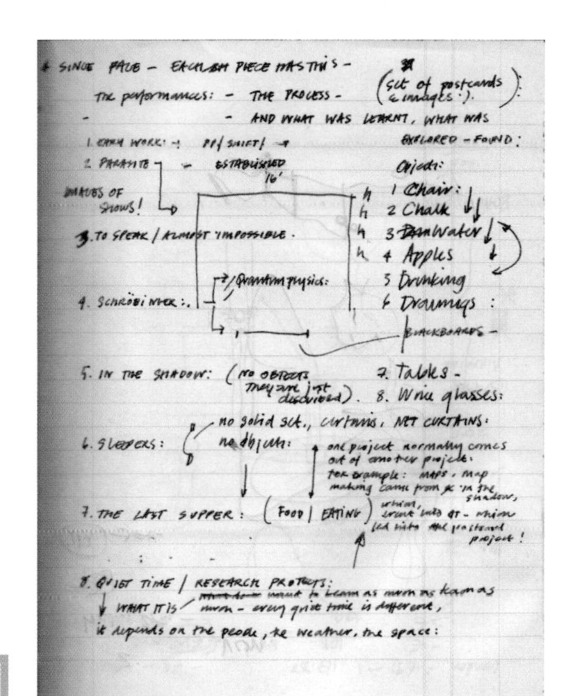

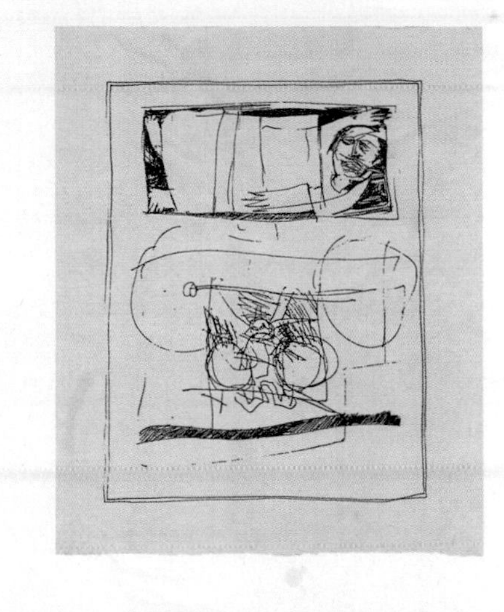

CHAPTER 1

RECKLESS SLEEPERS

'Reckless Sleepers' began in 1988 as the title of a Theatre Design degree performance at Nottingham Polytechnic conceived, devised and designed by Mole Wetherell and Michael Charlton. After graduation they created 'Tasting Black Wine', under the name 'Reckless Sleepers' (with Ian White and Natalie Keegan) based upon Angela Carter's novel 'The Magic Toyshop'. In 1989 Mole joined Station House Opera as a performer while continuing to develop his own work. 'Push Parallel' (made in collaboration with Debbie Stubbs and later Julie Harris) was performed at the International Mime Festival in London in 1991.

Barry Protheroe from Angel Row Gallery in Nottingham and David Metcalfe, who at that time ran Contemporary Archives in the city, expressed an interest in supporting a new project. Mole's proposal, 'Parasite', was influenced by the large cockroaches with which he shared his London flat. Although the gallery was not keen and the project was put to one side, they commissioned him to make 'Shift' (1992), a sculptural performance that made use of 5000 hardback books. The following year Mole left Station House Opera to work more or less full time with Reckless Sleepers.

Reckless Sleepers has experimented with various operating models but is now established as an organisation that supports Mole Wetherell's ideas. Although not a collective or ensemble along the lines of other leading contemporary performance companies, a significant contribution is made by company artists and technical personnel. Some, like performer Tim Ingram, have worked with the company for many years. Theatre is invariably a collaborative venture and Mole works with others to realise projects in various forms, including installation, exhibition, CD ROM, participatory, educational, durational, and sound projects.

The company has its administrative base in Nottingham and whilst active in the UK, has a developing profile across Europe and beyond. Mole Wetherell himself lives in the Belgian city of Gent.

Although Reckless Sleepers' work is informed by ground rules it does not work to an artistic policy. In common with the DOGME 95 'Vow of Chastity', the company attempts to reflect the time and place in which a piece is made and features of a particular space are often incorporated.

Reckless Sleepers' spatial design encompasses the entire performance space and minimises the distinction between 'on' or 'off' stage areas. For the reworking of 'GB Bill' at London's South Bank Centre on the fourth of July 1999 the company used a small platform five metres above ground level that forms part of the Royal Festival Hall. Different levels and platforms are a feature of the piece. This version of 'GB Bill' incorporated American themes and histories and was thus both site and date specific.

In Geneva for 'The Last Supper' we occupied a large hall. Beyond our performance space was a kitchen through a series of shuttered doors, left open for the start of the performance. Once all were settled the chef (Tina Carter) and two of the performers locked these doors, a choreographed sequence that sounded like prison doors being slammed shut. This act created a sense of beginning, more appropriate than the conventional rising of a curtain. We wanted people to see the kitchen, the food being prepared and encourage the sense that 'we know that this is going to happen'.

Attention to detail enhances the consistency and integrity of a work. Based around food and eating 'The Last Supper' features, among many others, Bobby Sands (who died whilst on hunger strike) and Elvis (who over-ate). Leonardo da Vinci is also represented because he painted the most famous version of 'The Last Supper'.

With 'GB Bill' we had quickly found a form for making and presenting work. It's a very time consuming process, the billboards themselves took weeks to construct. We didn't simply do the same show again and again. I like to adapt the performance to make it right for the space and time in which it takes place. In 'The Last Supper' this happens a lot, giving the work another layer, another dimension, which can lead to further narratives.

Multiple narratives are generated by performers and the people who witness the work. During a performance each performer will take a journey, and themselves take objects on journeys, in which they become vulnerable and open to possible change. However despite moments of catharsis it remains arguable whether meaningful change ever takes place. Systems are represented in which all are implicated and from which none may escape.

The company's aesthetic and philosophical roots appear firmly planted in European existentialism. Its work is human, in both scale and imagery, and expresses human experience from joy and elation to confusion, loss and grief. Frequent references are made to knowledge and betray a genuine fascination with culture, both historical and contemporary.

Reckless Sleepers' style of performance finds its reference points in TV, film and football. An alienation effect, disruptive of theatrical illusion, is created by means of an emphasis upon physicality over the constructed subtleties of character. No pretence is made at 'being' someone else, the performers are themselves. Mole wearing a bear suit in 'Spanish Train' (2006) is simply Mole in a bear suit. Even in the 'The Last Supper' (2004) in which references to larger than real life characters abound, there is no attempt at characterisation, merely signifying mannerisms or characteristics, such as the lowered gaze of Lady Diana.

The performers use an active and consistent performance mode, comparable with Michael Kirby's (1987) concept of 'received acting', in which they are seen to be involved in the onstage scenes as themselves, not 'playing' characters. Throughout a performance awareness of an audience is implicit and yet direct address is used sparingly. Within the space talking retains ambiguity and adds to the sense of the consistency of the 'other world' being observed.

Reckless Sleepers' work is conceived as both theatre and visual art. The company's approach reflects Hans-Thies Lehmann's notion of 'post-dramatic theatre' in which spoken text is simply one among many contributing systems. This is in contrast to traditional forms of theatre in which text is typically serviced by other systems. Each element, be it object or movement, is included on the basis of its relationship with the whole. When it was suggested that a small reading lamp with a cord pull might be introduced in 'Schrödinger's Box' it was recognised that an inspection lamp already in the piece does for various kinds of light. A specific light stuck in one place would be a theatrical device and would neither take a journey nor be open to change.

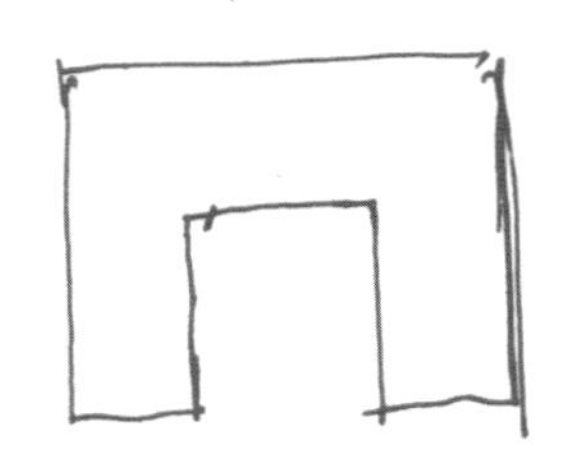

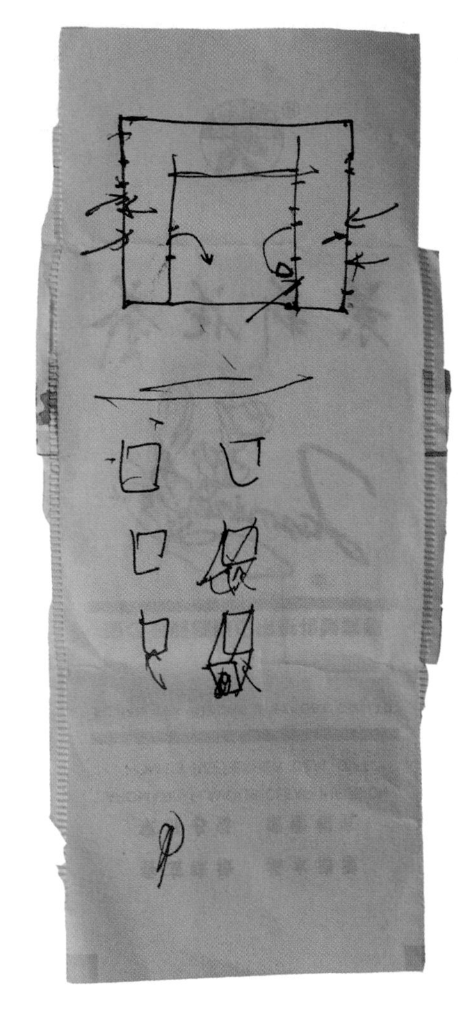

CHAPTER 2

'SCHRÖDINGER'S BOX'

'Schrödinger's Box' was built upon foundations laid down by 'Parasite' (1993), a performance that featured a determinedly physical brand of theatre within a collapsible set. Performed 90 times throughout Europe, impressions of 'Parasite' still resonate with those who witnessed it.

From 1995-1997 Mole concentrated on two large-scale projects, the development of a Nottingham rehearsal space ('N4' which became 'PreSet') and the production of 'Donkey' (which subsequently became 'Spion'), a large site-specific sound piece for the European Football Championships.

Having lost our first space through urban redevelopment I had to look for a new space and developed PreSet in 1996. which still exists today. PreSet was originally created as a space for the production of new work by various organisations. including Reckless Sleepers. It was the production base for 'Schrödinger's Box' as well as 'GB Bill'. 'Terminal'. 'In the Shadow'. the 'Millennium Projects'. and 'An illustrated guide to the 20th Century'.

'Schrödinger's Box' was made in several phases. In the first, in 1997, a 2-week period of research and development began with Tom Roden, Dan Belasco Rogers and Mole Wetherell, considering 'truth and lies'. The notion that when telling a lie the truth is also in your head led to research into Quantum Physics. Thought experiments, the means by which scientists explain complex concepts, were also investigated. Erwin Schrödinger's use of the image of a cat in a box to illustrate a superposition (see page 47), is a classic example of a thought experiment.

Subsequent phases saw the design of the set by Mole and Dan and further research. Formulas, scenes and speeches were pieced together, and the project's aims, goals, overall aesthetic, rules, ideas and imagery were identified. Scenes and scenarios were taken to a small working group and the design of the set was finalised.

Once constructed the company explored the set for an entire week. A period of rehearsal took place in which material was evaluated and re-written. A 50-minute version was performed as a work in progress at PreSet, and a further week was spent making use of the feedback received.

The project premiered at Alsager and began touring, during which aspects such as timing, choreography, journeys and performance qualities, were further developed. Positive feedback was received from fellow practitioners, audiences, programmers and the national and regional press. Although many were articulate about the work, it was apparent that some struggled with its content, perhaps expecting a stage version of 'Quantum Theory for Beginners', although it was never intended to popularise or explain science.

POSSIBLE PORTHOLES, DOORS, GATEWAYS:

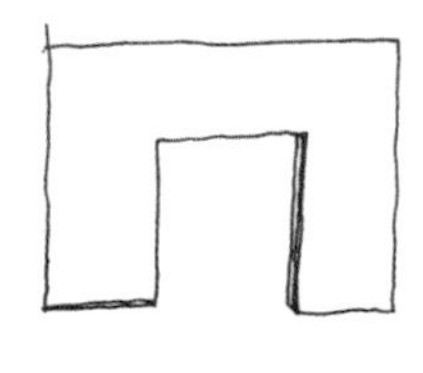

ARCH.

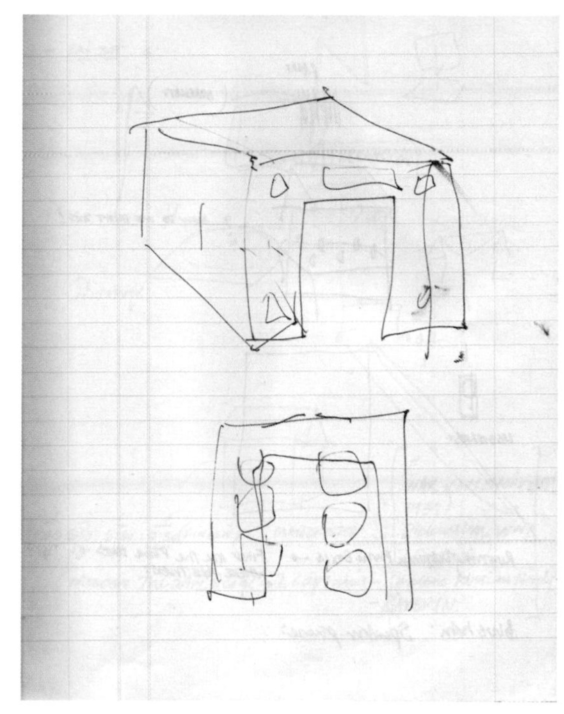

I think in some circles we were criticized for not explaining Quantum Theory. I'd like to say that we tried to make sense of it. and in our own peculiar way by presenting a piece that includes many aspects of Quantum Theory. We do explain these concepts. albeit not in a classical way. such as a lecture demonstration.

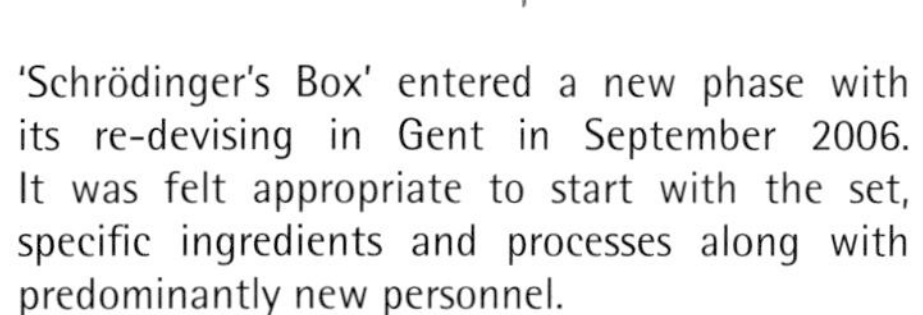

'Schrödinger's Box' entered a new phase with its re-devising in Gent in September 2006. It was felt appropriate to start with the set, specific ingredients and processes along with predominantly new personnel.

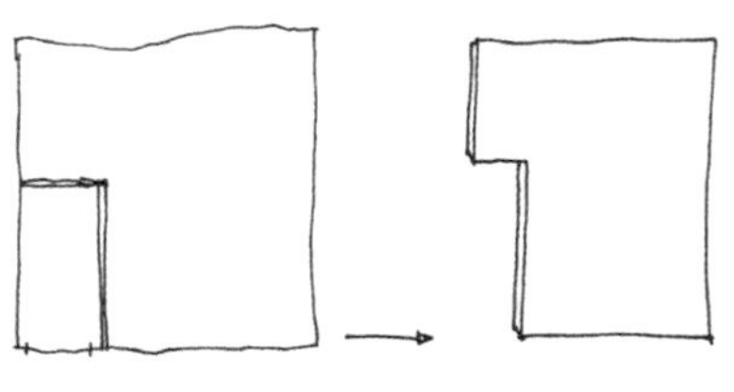

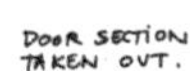

Working on the piece again has opened up a lot of questions. It is easier to adapt an existing work. expanding ideas. developing scenarios than to make something from scratch. Ideally I would like to spend at least another month simply looking at what the project was and what it can be. Even after spending a few days on it I had already drawn up a list of things I would like to reinvest my time in.

We re-opened the box. it had been closed but it has opened up a whole series of ideas. concerns. memories and reflections. It's difficult to close it again.

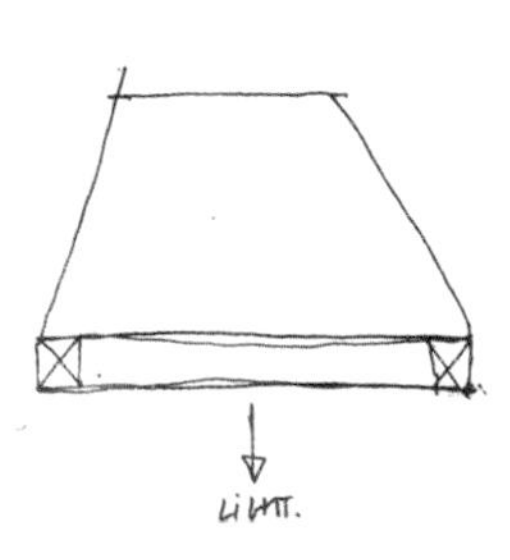

The box has the ability to timestretch, timetravel, magnify and incorporate the events of a specific place and time. We are observing it's peculiarities and deciding on it's function. Don't be afraid to pick up the bottle.

CHAPTER 3

The Box

1: It's like a travelling fairground ride, a mobile blood donor bus. It cannot speak itself; it is inanimate, however it enables others to speak. The box is a room. The box is a late night party.

The box is a hotel room. The one that we see is one of a multitude of boxes all stacked on top and to the side of each other, therefore the ceiling space and the corridor are the gaps in between each room and the sides are other boxes.

If you are being observed in the box, you are not aware of other things going on around you, they influence you but you don't know why. Ordinary, classical physics doesn't work properly in the box. Time does not work properly or in a linear way. We can see things getting stuck like a record - stuck and repeated so that a force, a thump, has to shift events on. The repeats become less clear, fuzzy, distorted.

It is never sunny, no natural light enters, no fresh air. You have to wear a special kind of suit or you're affected by its power.

2: A place removed from any specifics like time, location. (A Tardis?) Why are we there? Because we want to be, have to be. Whether this is our world that we inhabit, that changes guises, or a place of work. The box itself is anything we want it to be, what it needs to be for our own collective purposes. It and we are self-contained.

The box serves us as a means to an end. Once what is necessary from it is discovered, it is left or destroyed.

A place of confusion, questions, reciprocation, dislocation, replication. Secrecy, magic, complications and ignorance. Do we bring all this to it? Does it only exist because we are in it? Or is it in actual fact only a structure made of wood?

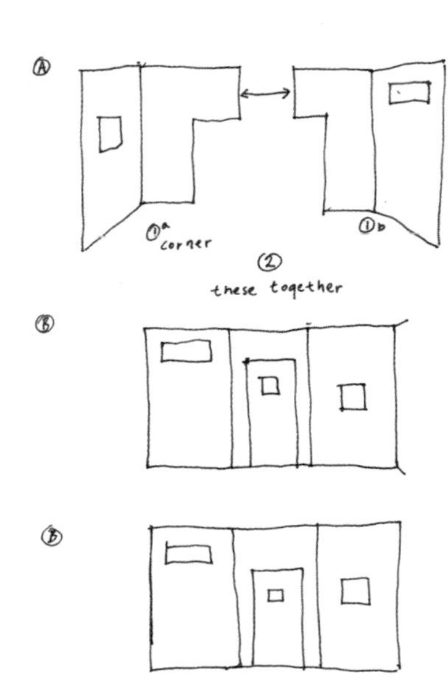

3: The box is an experimental chamber, a cloud chamber, a crucible, an alchemical experiment, a television, a radio, a tuning device it is so blank it calls other rooms into being. It is a psychological test to see what room you create out of the blankness. It is like a sensory deprivation room where at first you see nothing then your imagination takes over. It is a shelter from the elements. It is a deep level particle accelerator miles beneath the earth. It is a radio telescope control room. It is our last best hope. It's where Max Planck first thought of discontinuous energy. It's a figment of the imagination of a great man, his thoughts are so powerful, we have to act them out. It's for observing different rooms at different times. It's the 1927 conference hall at Solvay.

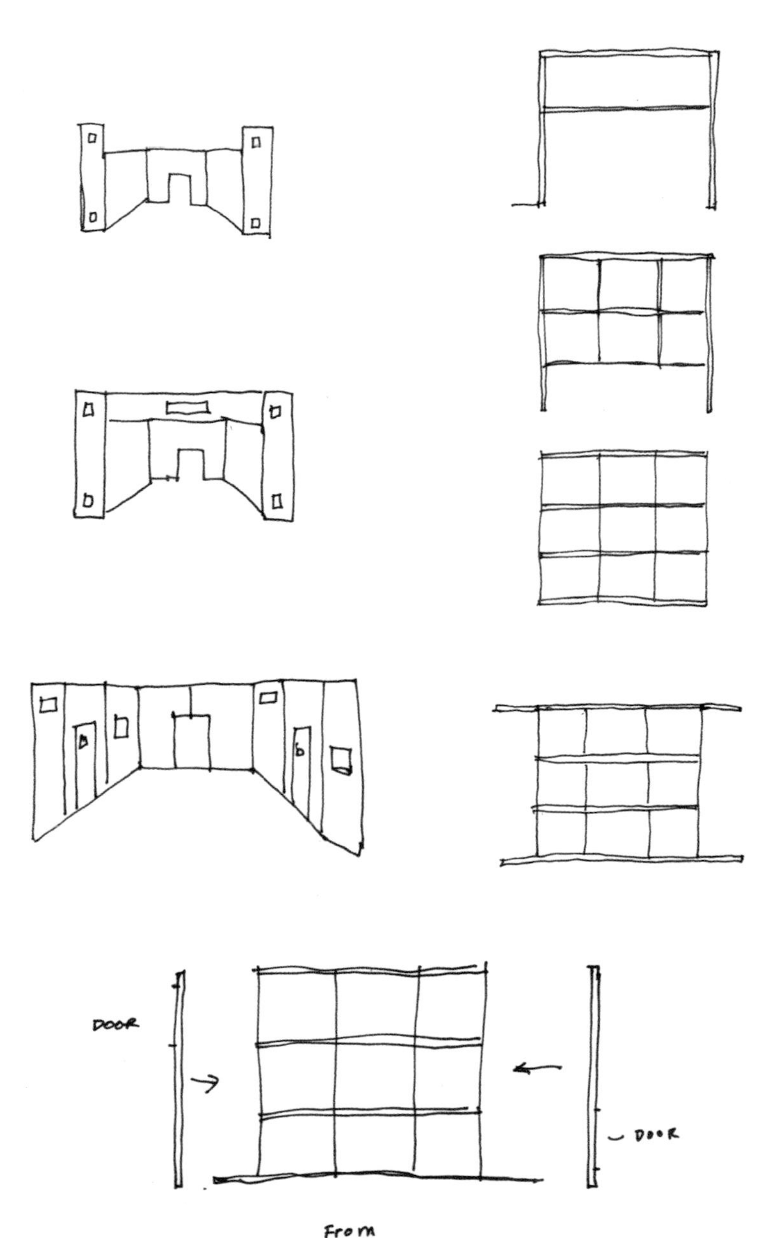

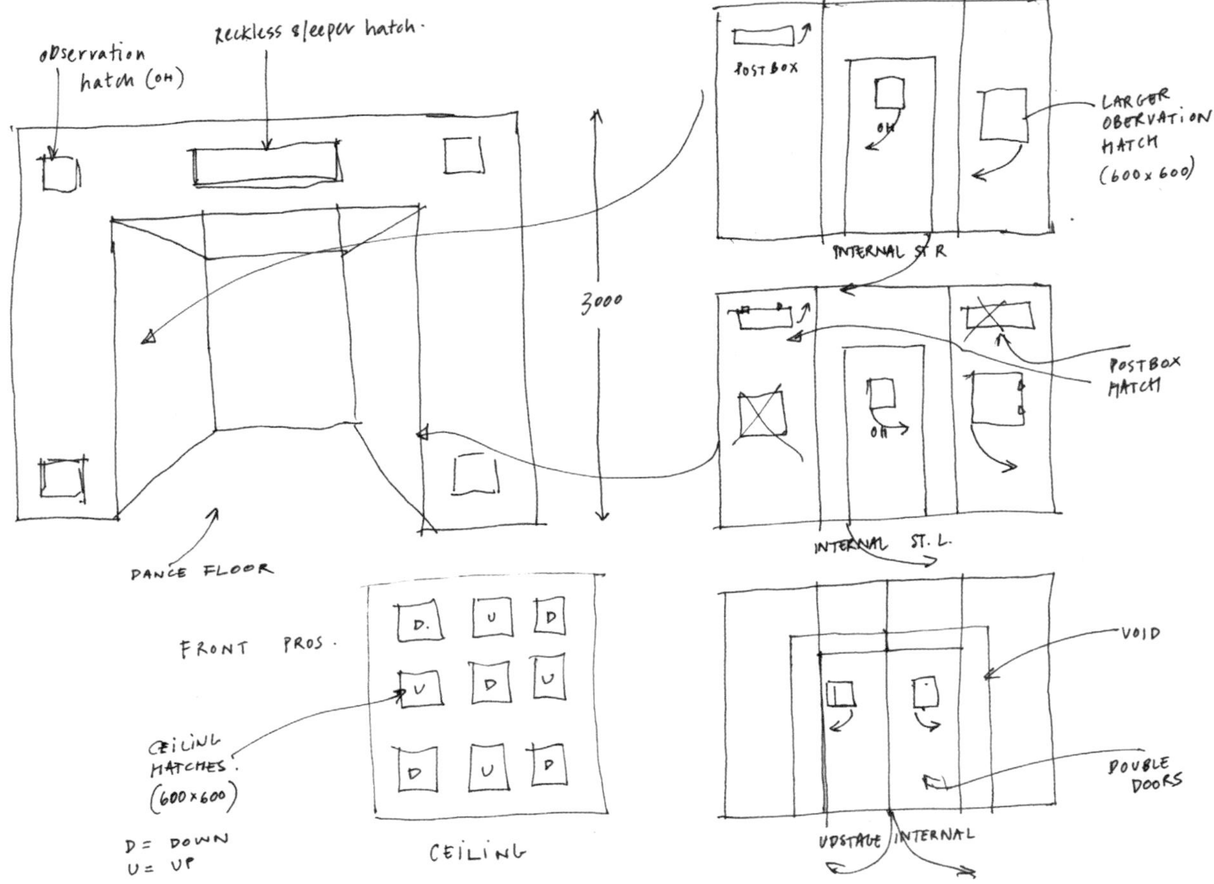

Everything has been extracted from the chamber. It is locked within miles of concrete lined with lead and porcelain. The only thing that can enter is thought. One by one we have introduced objects into this experiment in order that the thoughts have somewhere to be set down, otherwise they are too fleeting and we can't examine them. The power of it now is such that one is irresistibly possessed upon entering with material collected during this imaginative speculation. However it is by no means clear what material is and it is our task to observe, document and theorise; to try to tease out the common strands and arrive at laws. Laws of being, laws of imagination, equations for desire, memory, forgetfulness.

It's a dream factory. These people have come together to make material for other peoples' dreams; for insomniacs or the unimaginative. They have been selected for the extraordinary quality of their imaginations and creativity and have the task of making fantasy. It exhausts them and leaves them empty and confused and so they must be very carefully looked after.

It's very important that everyone thinks positively, for a negative or critical thought in this environment is magnified by the equipment and is potentially life threatening.

4: Never enter or exit the space across the line of the front edge. Events are magnified in the hatches at the front. Sleepwalkers' thoughts are also spoken from these hatches. The sides are constantly written on with graffiti. The doors and hatches in the inner chamber are for observation. As a scientist you may not enter the space once an experiment is in progress. You may observe from the ceiling hatches or use them to introduce new objects or take others out. The top hatch is exclusively for the Reckless Sleeper.

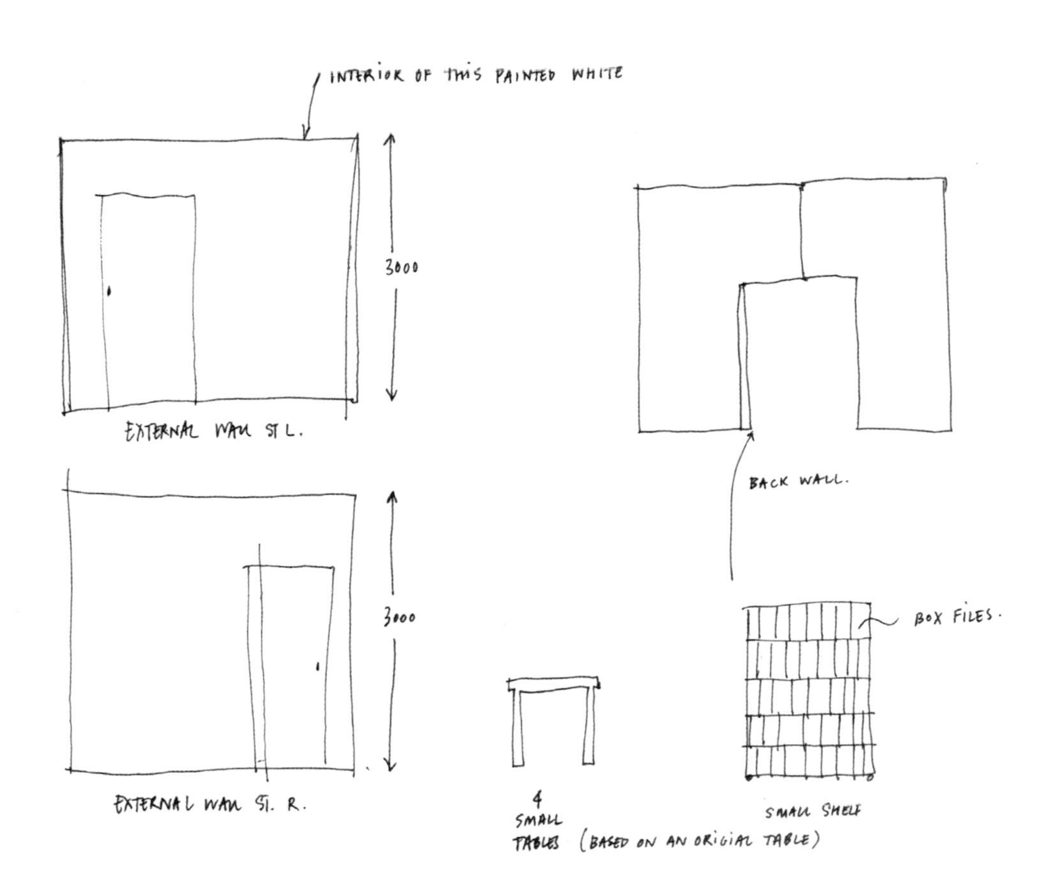
INTERIOR OF THIS PAINTED WHITE
3000
EXTERNAL WALL ST L.
3000
EXTERNAL WALL ST. R.
BACK WALL.
BOX FILES.
4
SMALL
TABLES (BASED ON AN ORIGIAL TABLE)
SMALL SHELF

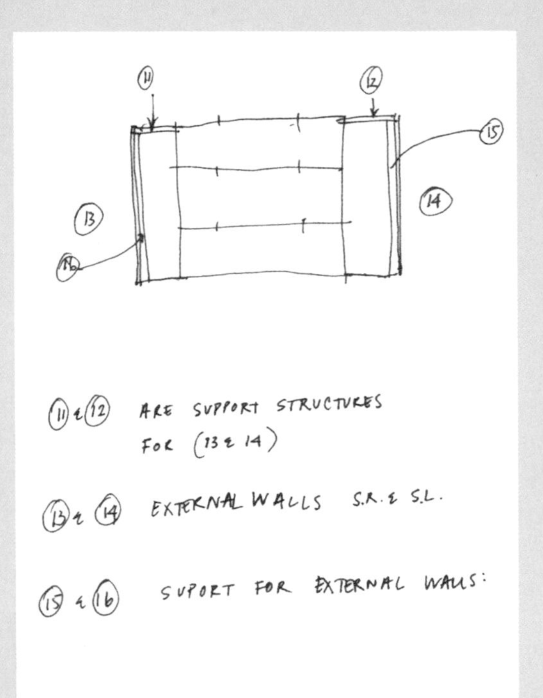

The box conceived by Erwin Schrödinger (refer to Page 44) is an enigma. Until it is opened and its contents observed, the cat within remains with its potential states superposed, both alive and dead. Reckless Sleepers took this virtual site of tension and designed a machine for performance, constructed from plywood and steel. What it contains is observable, unlike its predecessor, as a wall has thoughtfully, and in keeping with theatrical tradition, been removed.

The set resembles a basic childhood model theatre with proscenium, entrances and exits from both sides and the rear double doors. The positioning of hatches and objects enhance its apparent depth. What is within exists in various superposed states as multiple interpretations and potential narratives collide.

It could be imagined as an adventure playground, against which one can test strength and flexibility, as much mental and emotional as physical. It could be seen to demand strength of content and energy although the company's approach is subtle, in both concept and movement. Its design seems to focus attention onto the smallest gesture.

Nevertheless its physical properties still have to be understood and appreciated; the shape, size, weight of its doors and hatches, how best to scale its walls, to negotiate its many surfaces and angles. It becomes a trap for the unwary; in its current state its ceiling hatches are liable to fall open, swinging dangerously on their hinges. This creates a tension, a way of moving.

The physical relationship between performer and audience is inscribed in the spatial design of the set that occurs early in the process of making a work.

> I need to know early on the relationship the audience has to the performer. how the spaces are divided or brought together.

The Threatened Assassin
- Magritte (1927)

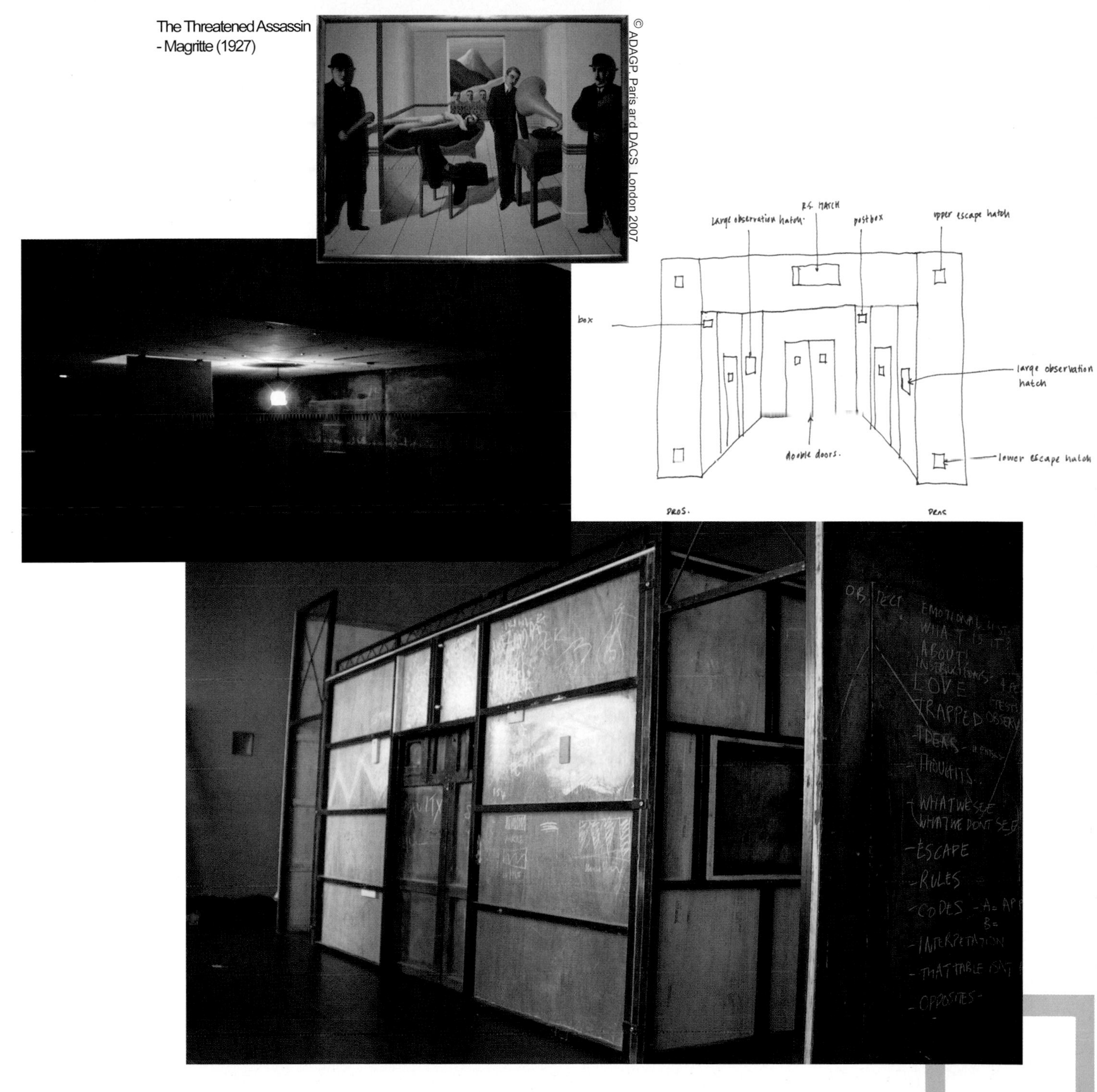

Mole's training in theatre design influences the ways in which the company understand and utilise space. The set of 'Schrödinger's Box' has a ceiling and a roof, unconventional elements in theatrical design and supposedly difficult to light. However one need not assume that the only source of light is from above. The interior is lit from the front by floor lamps, a series of overhead lamps (Parcans) illuminate the roof section, hatches acting as barn doors. Colour is limited to a blue (112) and green (114). Two portable inspection lamps are also used in sections of the performance.

In keeping with company principles the set is based upon straight lines and right angles. Natural perspective is used throughout, not the false variety found in many theatrical sets. This might explain why the forced perspectives of de Chirico seem less appropriate to the devising process than those of Rene Magritte. 'Schrödinger's Box' is a proscenium arch designed for a proscenium arch space, a box within a box.

This set of 'Schrödinger's Box' subsequently informed the design of 'In the Shadow' that featured a large wall containing hatches and other surprise elements. Despite its apparent solidity this was mounted on castors and allowed movement in relation to the wider performance space, the performers and the auditorium.

The set is not an artwork designed to appear in a gallery (interesting though that might be) but a machine for the generation of ideas and behaviours. Changes and adaptations, where possible, inspire new narratives.

I'd want to be able to lift it off the ground. Every little detail to be rethought. every hatch to be soundproofed.

ORDER OF ASSEMBLY.

notes.

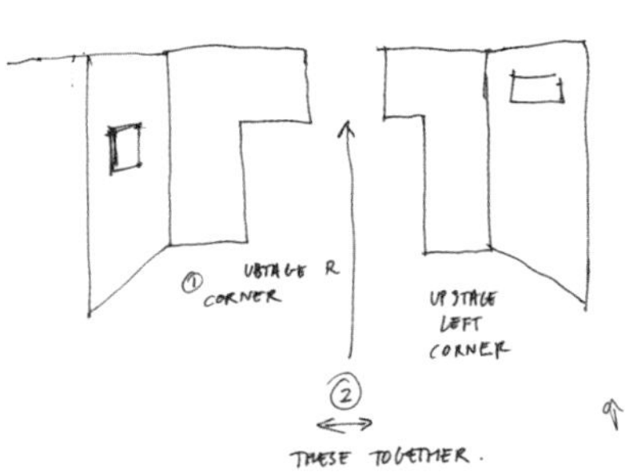

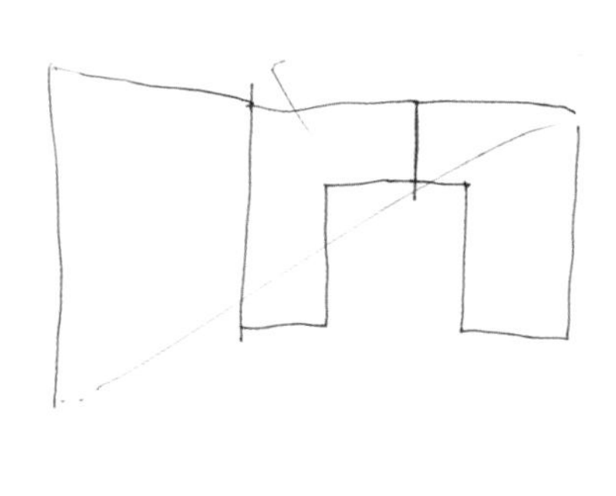

BACK

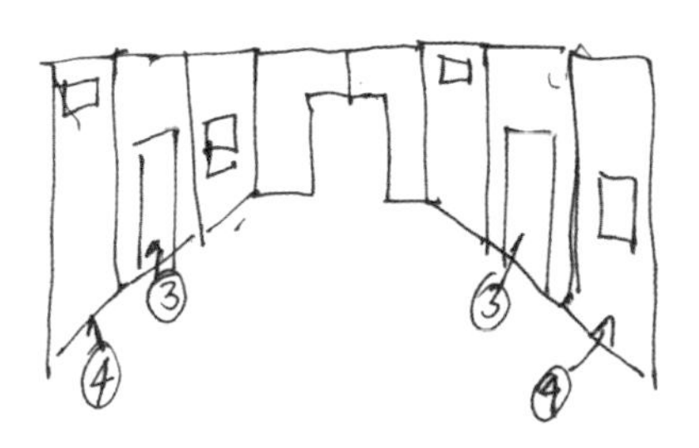

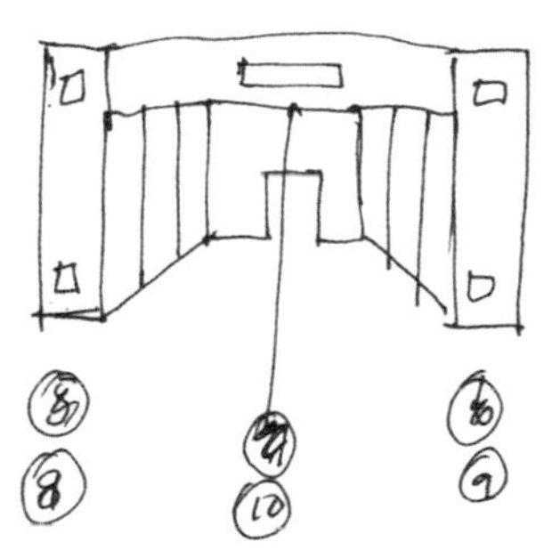

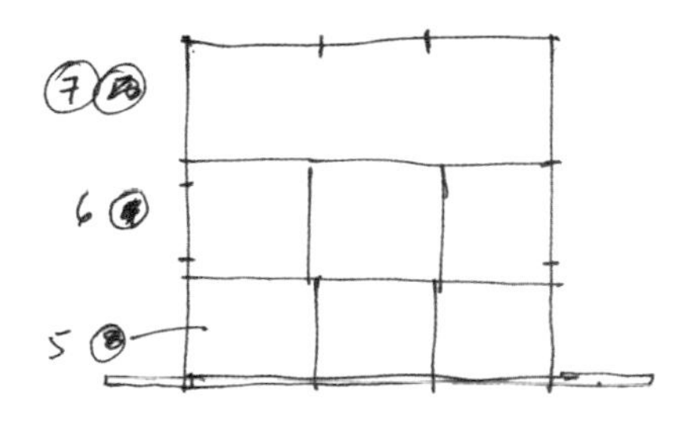

FROM ABOVE

ceiling hatches from above.

In advance of the re-devising in September 2006 the roof of the set was remade into nine sections instead of three, to make it stronger and easier to transport. The new wood had different properties to the original, being noticeably heavier and with a different texture.

Further adaptations might include the introduction of a wooden floor to better differentiate the box from the stage. Such a floor could also be drawn upon and include further hatches or a trap door.

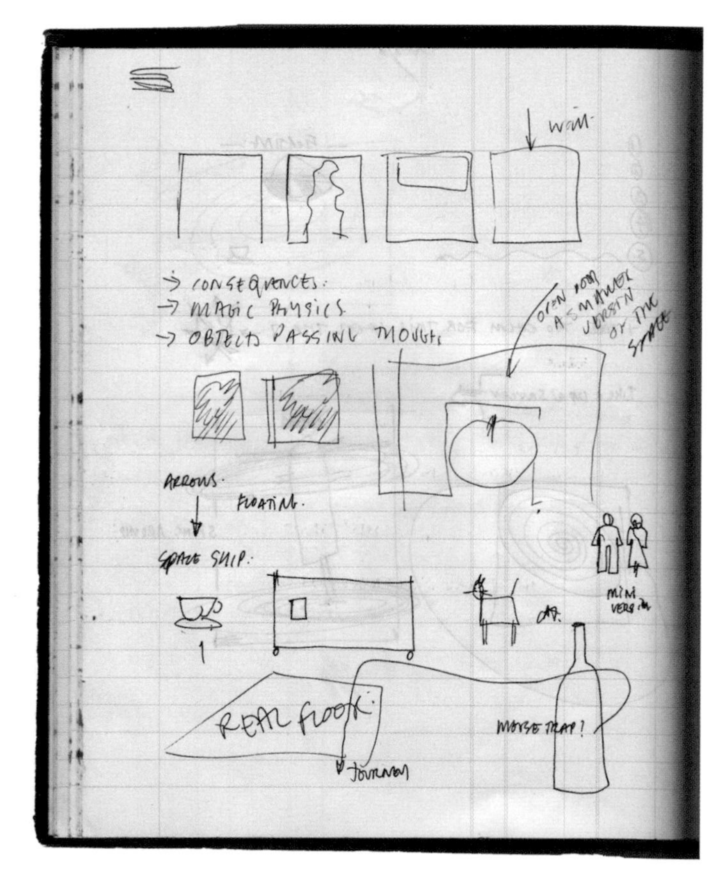

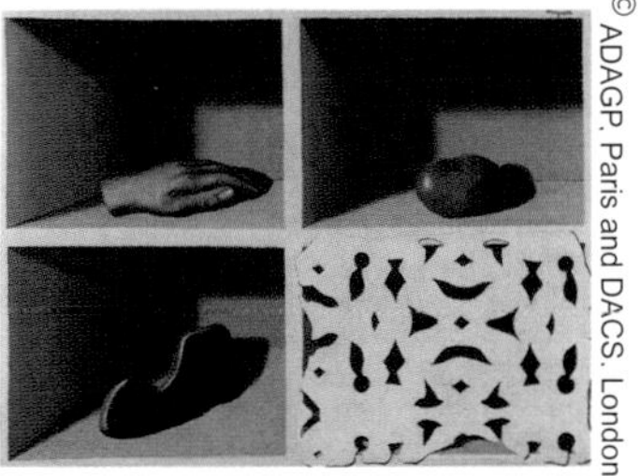
The Museum of a Night - Magritte (1927)

The Listening Room - Magritte (1958)

Blackboards, chalk and charcoal have become company 'trademarks' or signatures and play an integral part in the process of making. They are a means of making patterns, producing images and literally being 'graphic'. The notion of sharing a process, leaving a trail and a residue, is a feature of Reckless Sleepers' work. In 'Spanish Train' feathers/snow are allowed to settle on the floor and Leen Dewilde leaves a path through them, a symbolic path through the woods.

I think we need to know what things are available to us. I'm not interested so much with having video projections. It's too new. Perhaps a Super 8 film. an old-fashioned wind up gramophone. or a man playing the saw. Although we are looking at a miniscule quantum world. clockwork mechanics also feel appropriate.

Chalk has specific qualities leaving traces on skin and clothes as much as on blackboards. Blackboards themselves are low maintenance, versatile and flexible, ideal for mapping, and testing things out. Movement can affect what is written across its surface and further layers overwrite and obliterate.

Technology becomes useful only when meeting the needs of the person using it. Tools and opportunities exist that would until recently have been prohibitively expensive and/or difficult to achieve. But there is a risk of technology breeding dependency and limiting one's creative palette, or even becoming the most important feature of a work. Theatre is especially prone to seduction by novelty and spectacle. Artists are led by ideas, in turn driven by feelings and experience, not technology. Technology is itself led by ideas.

Christopher Bannerman (2004), Head of the Centre for Research into Creation in the Performing Arts (ResCen) has highlighted the relationship between 'the intuitive' and the 'disciplinary framework', which allows 'the inspirational insight greater scope, or... significance'.

I consciously wanted to introduce new people to the process of 'Schrödinger's Box'. It had to move on. Elsewhere in this book I describe Mathematics as an important factor in making work. For this process of redevising an old piece of work the number of people who didn't know 'Schrödinger's Box' outweighed those who did. Our (Mole and Tim's) memories were restricted to what we knew from performing it, and from watching video recordings. We had no idea, and there is no record of the journeys taken by Marie, Jake and Sarah. But I didn't just want to resurrect it. With this ratio it was possible that things would move on, things would change.

She's waiting for something to happen – no she can't stand still:
She has to stand still:
No movement,
You have to stay in this space & do nothing:
Do Nothing / Do Nothing at all:

What:

I'd like to know why your feet don't touch the ground!
I'd like to know why you're smiling.
I'd like to know how doing nothing means doing so much!
I want you to run in the space, I want you to fall over, I want you to try and stay still and count to 100, I'd like you to close your eyes and imagine that all the objects are spinning inside this room.
I'd like you to understand that gravity doesn't work the same way here as it does there.
~~td~~ I want you to know that

CHAPTER 4

WAYS OF WORKING

The reaction between intuition and its framework can generate considerable energy and encourage conceptual leaps. On experiencing an artwork one may on occasion be inspired to ask silently, 'How did you do that?' Or even more rarely – 'how did you think of doing that?' Sometimes artists fail but such is life. Among art forms, performance places the artist in an especially vulnerable position, but the performance artist likewise has the potential to deeply affect those who witness them. Experiencing 'Parasite' simultaneously opened up conceptual and physical space. Artists have the capacity to take us to places within our own imaginations that we barely knew existed.

Each of the artists who work with Reckless Sleepers brings their own character and way of working. Each is expected to make a real contribution in the development of material. Devising is a rigorous process that requires experience, understanding of process and context, along with highly evolved conceptual skills. All are mutually dependent upon one another's creativity.

In the re-devising of 'Schrödinger's Box', the artists' (Mole Wetherell, Tim Ingram, Leen Dewilde and Ine Naessens) asked questions of the original work, and generated new ideas. The involvement of new people is necessary because new ideas are necessary. Even within fixed ensembles there remains a need for external involvement.

Reckless Sleepers seems, like all performance companies, to work with a particular style of performer. Artists are invited into projects on the basis of their individual traits and the aesthetic of a specific piece of work. 'The Last Supper', despite dealing with harrowing subject matter, demands an upbeat performance style. 'Schrödinger's Box', on the other hand, demands performers with what can be best described as 'an aura of sadness'. One identifies with certain performers as they undergo their journey through a performance. Within overtly physical or durational work, empathy can be generated directly through being in the presence of another human being under duress.

Mole as Creative Director must pay attention to fine detail whilst not losing sight of the evolving bigger picture relating to all work in repertoire, under development, or as yet unformed. Direction involves communication, the management of people, active observation, depth of thought and clarity of expression. It involves feeling as much as seeing which material and scenes to push and which to let go.

In 1997/8 Dan Belasco Rogers took the role of the 'outside eye' with Mole as the inside performer/director. In the re-devising, despite no outside eye being involved, it was possible for Mole to step out by substituting another person in the space or by getting 'in' to illustrate. Whereas standard practice might be to shout something along the lines of 'It's not working, try...' Mole's approach allows performers to finish and often to try again.

This can yield results that are more developed, as well as helping to maintain momentum. Different contexts call for different directing styles; as work becomes more fixed the need for discipline seems to grow. But overall the company's approach is increasingly based upon self-direction, augmented by post-rehearsal and post-show discussions.

(DAN) NOTES + IDEAS.

1.Drink/Drunk	Find a way into Drink/Drunk and out of it. Use Jake's equivalents rule again.
2.Forest meets "we keep missing".	Do the paths in the forest dictate flows through, and repeat we keep missing.
3.Briefcases.	Make an intricate choreography of paths and briefcase.
4.Dustcovers over everything!	
5.Marie disappears vertically through hatch.	She is on an "ariston" journey which gets more and more elaborate with objects placed in the way until finally she walks up to one table and disappears. (someone immediately sits at to do some action.)
6.Close Up/Far away.	Two people sit opposite each other and finally kiss as through hatch, someone eats an apple very slowly at the same time.

NOTES /COMMENTS/IDEAS. (Dan).

Trying to find open hatches.
Feet on ground taboo.
Changing feeling of location.
Wendy House/ experimental. Sauna.
Pictorial motifs from Magritte - Sleeper seen through hatch. (Mole).

Scene moving across space at first just a task. Marie and Sarah passive. Mole and Dan pulling.

Development - Jake active, Sarah pouring drink for Jake who sort of becomes drunk because of crudity of movement.

Development - Marie and Tim not co-operating at table. Jake takes tablecloth - very different feeling.

Experimented on/Experimenters - Audience as participants.

Changing planes - using ladder as conveyance belt.

14

I love sitting inside theatre spaces. I love to sit and look at an empty space. it's the most peaceful place to invent and create new things. I especially find this on trains (I wrote this whole section on a train journey). But theatres have a special way of giving me inspiration.

Inside the theatre I always take a notebook. even if it's to see a performance. and some moment or action will make me think of something. another scene

It's rare in an end-on performance that we cross the divide into the auditorium. We invite people to share a space with us in 'Parasite' and 'The Last Supper' and we are really close in 'Spanish Train' but we don't cross into your space. I don't like it when it happens to me. I've been singled out in performances and although I'm a performer I'm petrified.

In our performances I've often considered myself an inside eye. a director. but on the inside. I think that the work moves much quicker when in this position. however as an outside eye I will always demonstrate what I mean on stage. I will watch things from the outside and make comments but it's normal that I will want to articulate these things physically. with my hands as if drawing things. In 'Schrödinger's Box' Dan was outside. I was inside and this worked.

I was in the original trio of 'The Last Supper' with Tim and Pascale (Petralia). I took time outside but now I'm in it again. It feels better to direct from the inside. With 'Spanish Train' I now get notes. Leen has the ability to see what I do and is consistent in what she does. It's what I've been doing all along. We now use a system of work in progress presentations to develop work. 'Spanish Train' had four of these. providing an opportunity for the input of tens of 'outside eyes' and of course we have a very critical articulate audience.

It's useful to have outside perceptions. In 'Spanish Train' Steve Slater from Tramway suggested that after I lose the bear outfit at the end of the snow scene I should carry on dancing. It works and we have kept it in.

I also squash or try to squash only one tomato in the picnic song and dance routine. And we've been able to give each other notes and direction in the touring of the piece.

When we perform we often try new things out. or accidents may happen (like the kettle in our first piece) which remain part of it. Structures remain. but every time a piece is performed we add something new.

In 'Schrödinger's Box' there is a scene where we grab Tim. take him through the corridor space and throw him into the exterior area stage right. In one performance because of the proximity of the door. I was able to hold him. open the escape mechanism and throw him outside onto the street. I still remember the sensation of cold air hitting me. In 'Spanish Train' I go for a walk. I leave Leen on her own. a crucial moment for me because it's uncomfortable for the audience (am I coming back?). I do. and the performance continues.

Each performer will have established an internal logic. to what. why. who. where and how they are on stage. I have details and images that occupy my mind as I'm going through the performance.

Observation needs to extend beyond the conventions of the performance frame, to include the performers' body language and asides. What might appear to be a weakness, such as a performer apparently lost within a section, may nevertheless result in a strong presence. Within systems that are seemingly out of control, a constant provides others something to play against.

I like mistakes, accidents, unintentional actions and misunderstandings that can affect a piece; I love to see Tim falling over. Accidents and mistakes are important to the development of ideas. This is how cornflakes happened, by accident.

For a small improvised scenario based around 'I'll be back in a minute' Mole used elephants ('1 elephant, 2 elephant') as a way of counting 60 seconds, a minute. Because she did not understand this detail Leen omitted it from her representation of Mole's improvisation. In Dutch *eenentwintig* does not have the same significance. The reference to elephants adds a surreal and potentially interesting layer to the work and demonstrates the potential for misinterpretation between languages.

I felt that this was the most interesting and humorous part of the scene. I said 'I'll be back in a minute' and you could hear me counting through to 60 and wonder 'which door is he going to come through?'

These mistakes or accidents form the pieces and this again illustrates for me why it is:
a) important to try things
b) keep an open mind in this part of the process
c) always keep the channels of communication open. I often overhear questions about the content or something. These are key parts of the process, because there may be something in the working out of an instruction that makes more or as much sense as the instruction.

One of the company's fundamental rules is that in devising all performers must practically demonstrate ideas to the rest of the group. An individual can readily succumb to the tendency of immediately negating an idea, but their view need not be final. Another person may take things from it, perhaps to a different context. By showing an idea it becomes 'real', ceases to be a thought and once articulated one is able to move on. The insistence upon showing is a reaction against the 'sitting around a table, talking about stuff' attitude prevalent in devising work. Not having a big table or a comfortable chair in the devising space also helps in this regard. Small tables and wooden chairs, with room for only one person can function as objects in the work. Talking about the work is done in a separate space so there is a division between work and having a break.

A long table is important for eating together. relaxing and talking about what we could do. and then we go into the rehearsal space to try it.

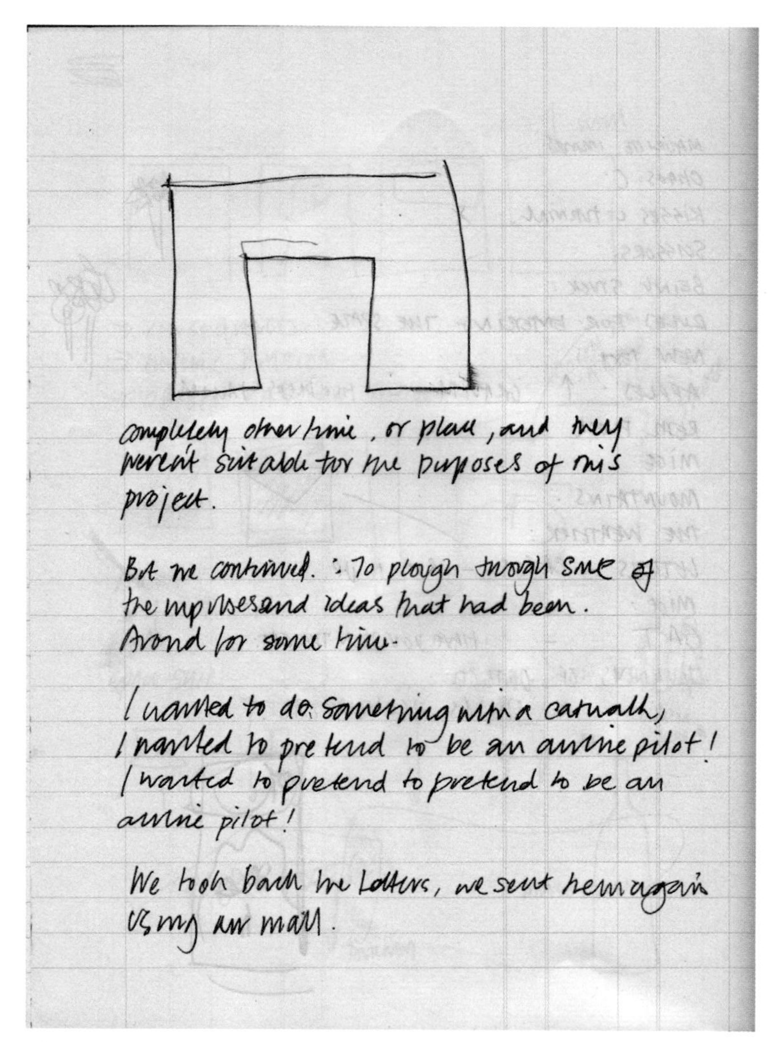
completely other time, or place, and they weren't suitable for the purposes of this project.

But we continued. To plough through some of the improvised ideas that had been. Around for some time.

I wanted to do something with a catwalk, I wanted to pretend to be an airline pilot! I wanted to pretend to pretend to be an airline pilot!

We took back the letters, we sent them again using air mail.

Reckless Sleepers' devising for performance involves working methodically through scenes, tasks and processes and recording these on video. A video camera functions like an outside eye and is a useful tool for identifying potential directional changes, although it is not used to fix a piece. Once a piece becomes established video is an important resource. Reviewing video material also provides confirmation of what has been achieved.

I'd like to be able to separately record every show. a camera following a person through their performance. or alternatively make notation of each performer's intentions and route through a piece. I think we are close to establishing this in our working practice.

Although there are no set routines and events do not appear particularly disciplined, a considerable amount of material is explored during an average day of devising.

At the time it feels frustrating that all of these ideas are generated and only a handful of them get into the performance. there's probably a formula or equation. like a day's worth of devising = 1 minute of the final presentation. It takes longer than we think. always...

Although strict organisation might seem desirable it simply cannot be this way in the early stages of a work, when channels need to be open, questions asked and attempts made to answer them. The nearest thing to an agenda in the re-devising was 'this is what we would like to look at today'. Being open to tangential ideas can lead to productive and previously unimagined situations.

The role of Creative Director involves negotiation and flexibility more than forward planning but being a performer/director presents difficulties in relation to allowing appropriate levels of 'time out' and 'time in'. By working 5 days to the performers' 4 or by working a full day and bringing the performers in after lunch, Mole can free up time in which to view video material, evaluate what has been done and consider what to try next. Within the tight time frame for the re-devising of 'Schrödinger's Box' there was little opportunity for 'time out' so instead, at the end of the fifth day, Mole wrote a series of lists in chalk on the external walls of the set.

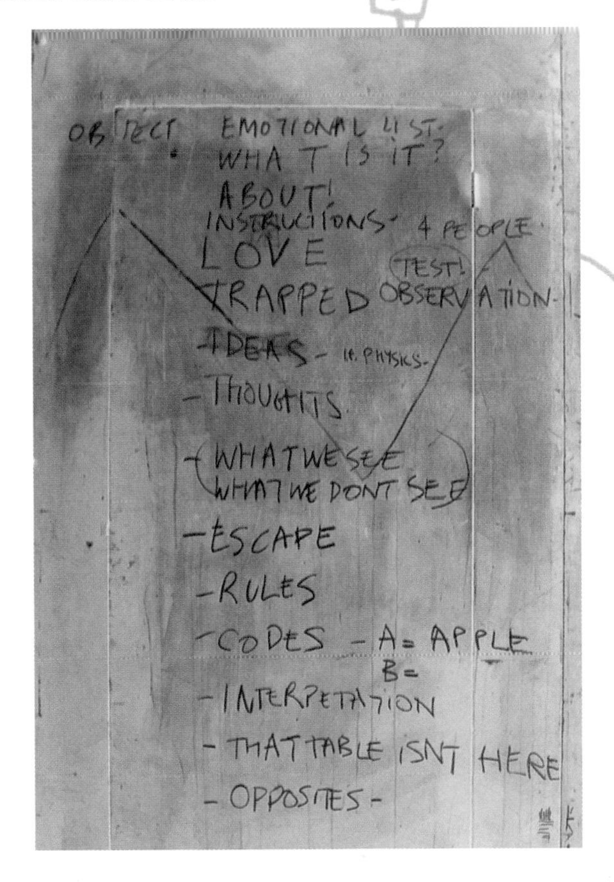

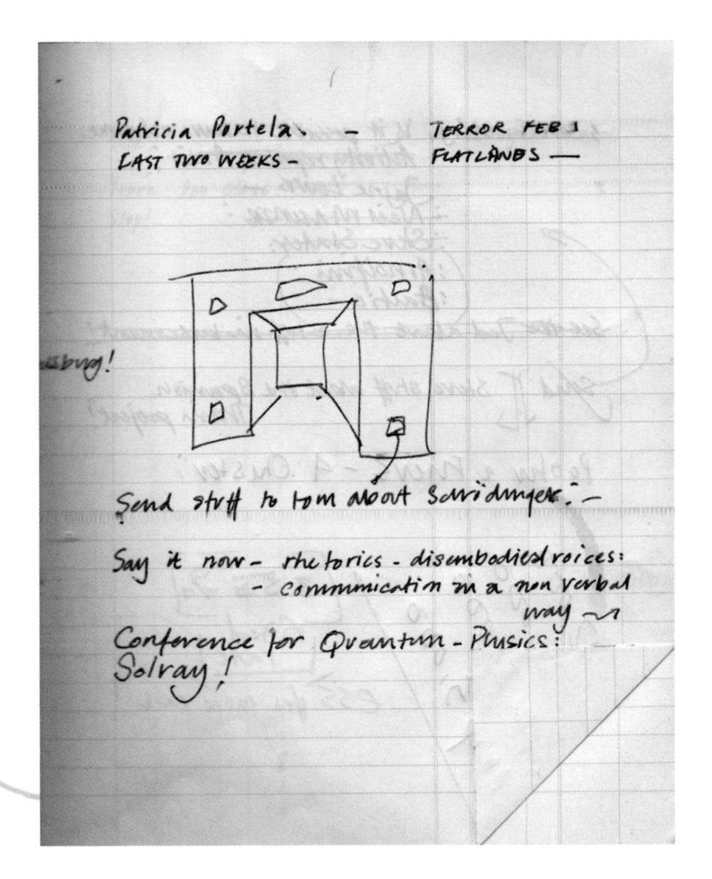

I felt a pressure to come up with something that provided the other members of the company with the next step ready for tomorrow. What I really needed was a day of quiet. a nothing day on my own with the blackboard and a notebook and a video to watch. This would normally be structured into the working practice but we were not making a piece. I felt that if I didn't come up with something the whole system inside the room would grind to a halt.

This was an attempt to clarify things and make them visible. take things out of the notebooks. out of my head.

I like its construction because it makes complete sense to me. The next phase is writing this down in my book. on a single page. so that I can see everything together.

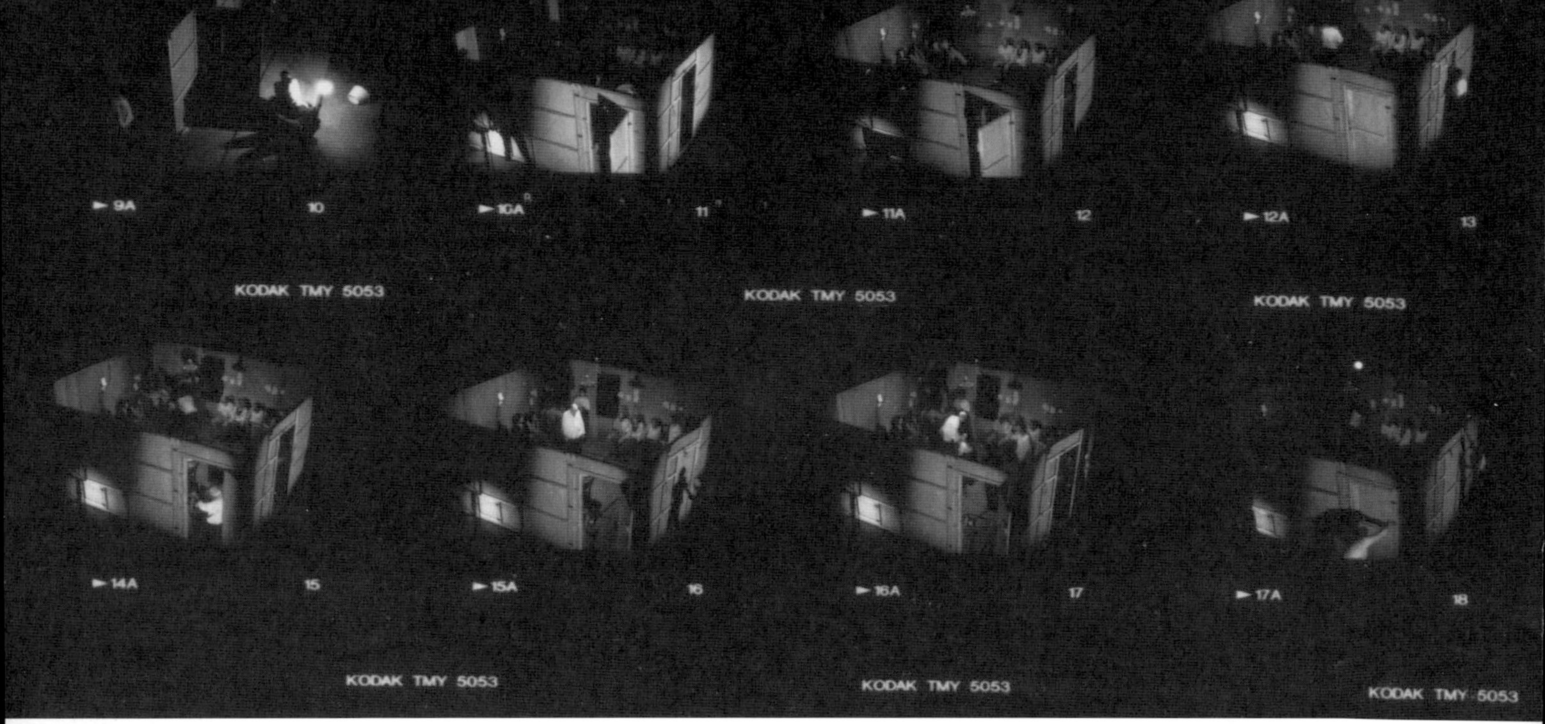

We try to establish the crux of an idea or a certain scene. so that it is not merely a three-minute section. an idea that has no journey or consequence. What we started to do with 'Schrödinger's Box'. and to an extent in 'Parasite' was pare everything to its bare bones. it's emotional content. and then to push this (singular idea) further.

In 'Parasite' the first presentation had a huge collection of ideas. thoughts and process. images and scenes. and what we (Dan and Mole) did was take it down to its essentials before expanding it. The singular idea took the form of the 'violence' scene. which was seen three times in the performance. from different points of view. The first took place outside. was heard but remained unseen. the second was only visible through a window. the third through the double doors and the fourth was seen by all. on the inside. 'Parasite' laid down a simple structural device. the same sequence of events being witnessed from different viewpoints.

People sitting in a particular spot see the action. or part of the action through this window. those sitting here can't see anything at all. but can hear the action taking place behind them. They look to one another for cues as to what might be going on and what they see is a real response.

The making of the 1988 'Reckless Sleepers' degree performance was structured around working every Tuesday and Thursday over 12 weeks with a group of 1st year Theatre Design students. This allowed plenty of time in between to shape ideas but despite the process remaining much the same over the years the time frame has shrunk.

Within these restrictions an alternative approach might be to devise without the full company. All might spend an initial 2 weeks together after which the Creative Director and a co-writer might go away and write the text and produce storyboards. The document could then be handed back to the rest of the company to work with.

'The Last Supper' developed out of a simple conversation and workshops that took place over a few days, after a lengthy period of historical and biographical research. The piece was written within 3 days and a document produced which formed the basis for future rehearsals. It was performed and rewritten during a further 2 week period with direction being given based upon a clear idea of role.

FAVOURITE BITS

A pleasurable but useful way of concluding a devising phase involves editing, by means of memory, things that have been experienced. In Gent the performers were asked to describe their favourite part of the space and to improvise their favourite moment(s).

In his reflection upon the philosophy of his friend Samuel Beckett, John Calder (2001, p.67) writes that 'A good memory cannot be very interesting because there is no contrast between what is significant and what is not. Everything can be recalled, and therefore there is no sense of discovery'.

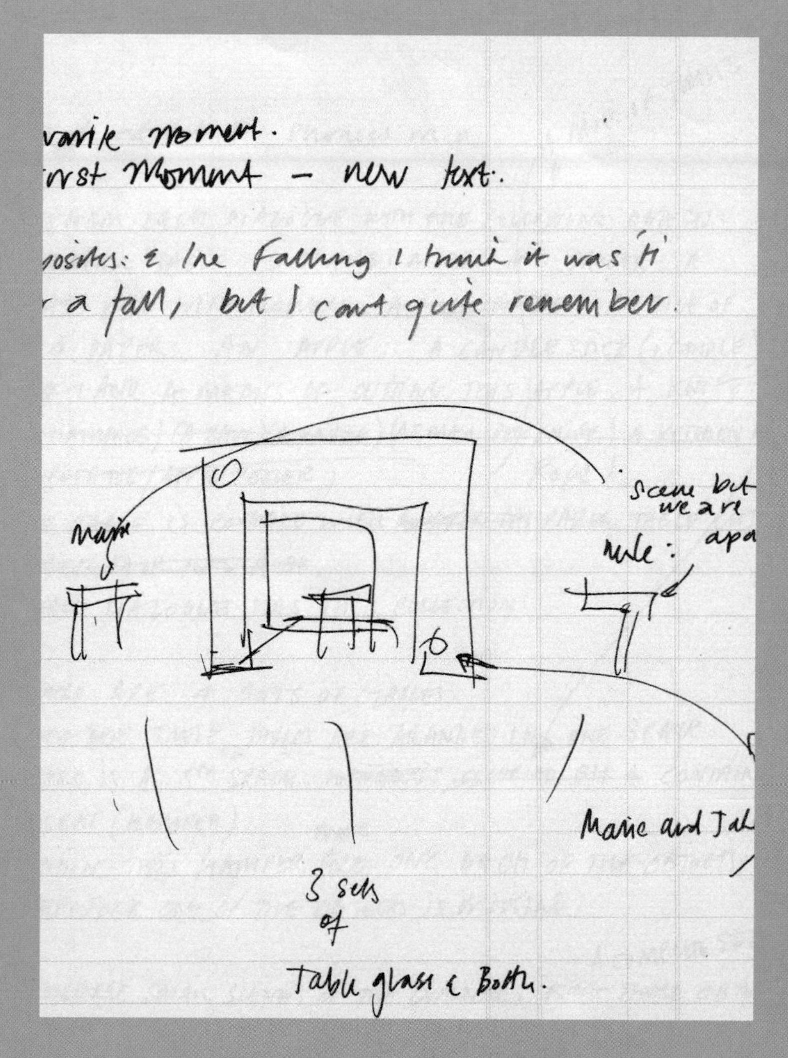

The artists' favourite bits were (in no particular order):

- First spaceship
- Hatch with heart drawn on
- Leen with rabbit ears
- The apple's successful escape bid
- The cup's 'magical' disappearance (by the person holding it simply turning around)
- Leen trying to smash an apple (with hammer)
- Tim pretending to be stuck in chewing gum
- The tone of Ine's voice shouting 'stop, move faster'
- Roughing up Mole's hair to resemble Einstein
- Tim falling with his legs remaining in the air

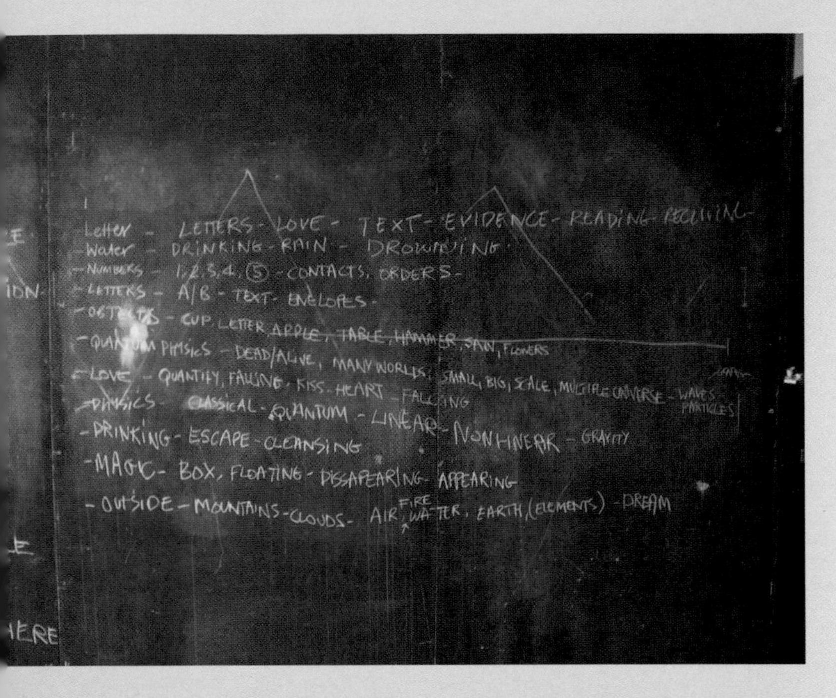
Letter - LETTERS - LOVE - TEXT - EVIDENCE - READING - RECEIVING -
- Water - DRINKING - RAIN - DROWNING
- NUMBERS - 1,2,3,4, 5 - CONTACTS, ORDERS -
- LETTERS - A/B - TEXT - ENVELOPES -
- OBJECTS - CUP, LETTER, APPLE, TABLE, HAMMER, SAW, FLOWERS
- QUANTUM PHYSICS - DEAD/ALIVE, MANY WORLDS, SMALL, BIG, SCALE, MULTIPLE UNIVERSE - WAVES PARTICLES
- LOVE - QUANTITY, FALLING, KISS - HEART - FALLING
- PHYSICS - CLASSICAL - QUANTUM - LINEAR - NONLINEAR - GRAVITY
- DRINKING - ESCAPE - CLEANSING
- MAGIC - BOX, FLOATING - DISSAPEARING - APPEARING
- OUTSIDE - MOUNTAINS - CLOUDS - AIR, FIRE, WATTER, EARTH, (ELEMENTS) - DREAM

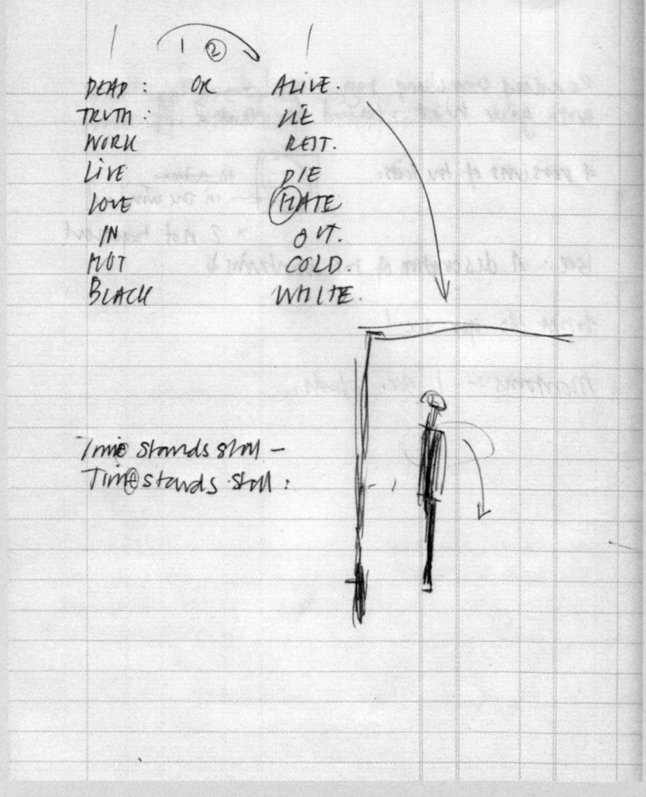
DEAD : OR ALIVE.
TRUTH : LIE
WORK REST.
LIVE DIE
LOVE HATE
IN OUT.
HOT COLD.
BLACK WHITE.
Time stands still -
Time stands still :

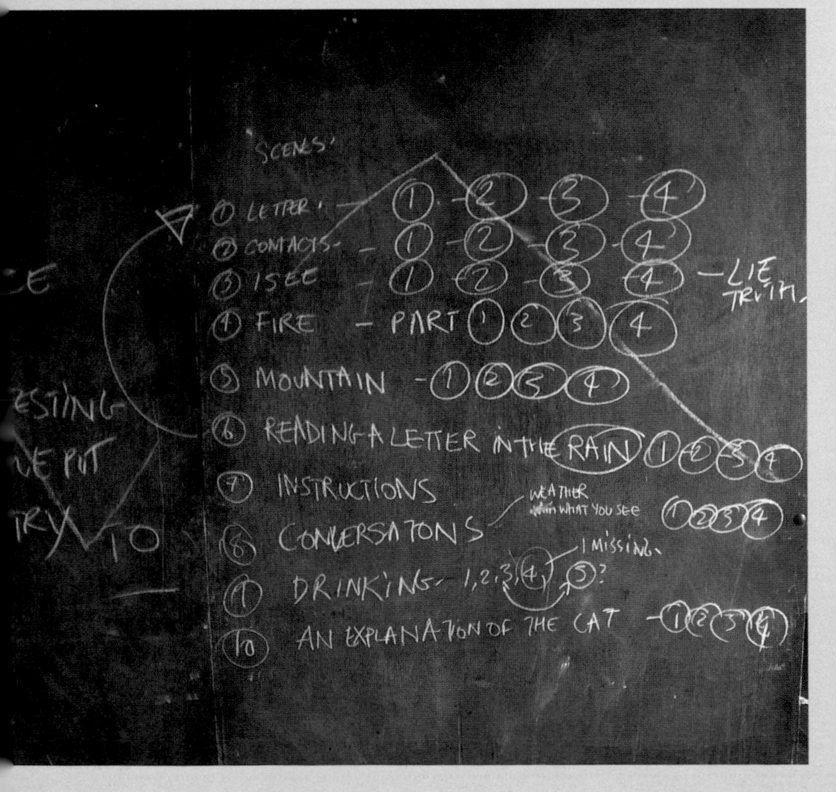
SCENES:
1 LETTER - 1 - 2 - 3 - 4
2 CONTACTS - 1 - 2 - 3 - 4
3 I SEE - 1 - 2 - 3 - 4 - LIE TRUTH
4 FIRE - PART 1 2 3 4
5 MOUNTAIN - 1 2 3 4
6 READING A LETTER IN THE RAIN 1 2 3 4
7 INSTRUCTIONS
8 CONVERSATIONS
WEATHER WHAT YOU SEE 1 2 3 4
9 DRINKING - 1, 2, 3, 4, 5?
1 MISSING
10 AN EXPLANATION OF THE CAT - 1 2 3 4

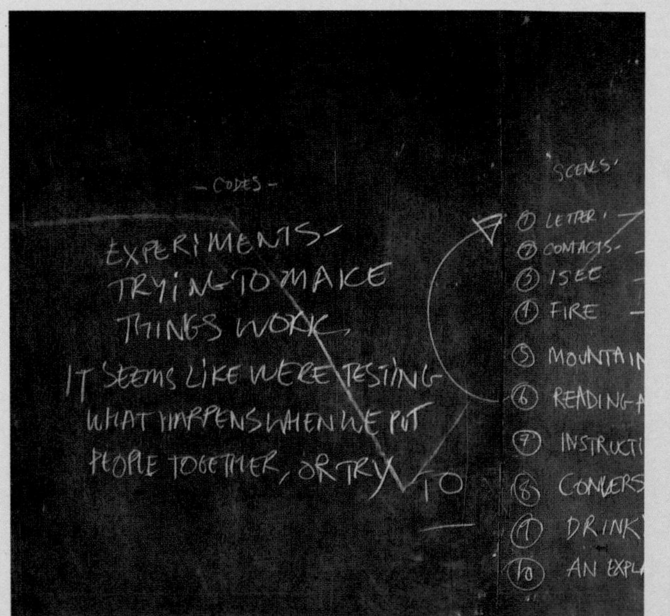
- CODES -
EXPERIMENTS -
TRYING TO MAKE
THINGS WORK
IT SEEMS LIKE WE'RE TESTING
WHAT HAPPENS WHEN WE PUT
PEOPLE TOGETHER, OR TRY TO
SCENES:
1 LETTER
2 CONTACTS
3 I SEE
4 FIRE

Mole's note: 1234 are the scenes that I need to find.
The spaceship of Star Trek has a question mark, as I don't know where it lives in this world.

A 'performer devising tool' or process
1) to do a task, as close to the request as possible. Performers are often asked to interpret an idea, so this should instead be about trying to do what is asked
2) to do it again with a specific intention, adaptation or idea "in mind".
3) Stage 1 gives room for other interpretations i.e. it is seen, and therefore can be pushed further. There are multiple directions that an idea can travel. Sticking to an originator's intention is crucial for this process to work
but
4) there should also be room for an idea, a mistake, an interpretation to move. For instance, a set of instructions in the process 'Consequences' that I gave to Ine, were interpreted in a very different way to how I had imagined when she interpreted 'corridor' as 'corner'. This made me see something different and was much more interesting than what I had imagined. What she presented was an honest response to a task that was more interesting than the intended outcome. It wasn't an attempt to be different; the task was attempted, as an honest response.

Honesty here is trying to really make what is asked. A dishonest response would be contrived or made to be clever. or what happens in my case by trying to make something funny.

NEGATIVE SPACE

The beginning – Outside the space – Normally we would present 'Schrödinger's Box' with enough space to the left of the box to perform what we call the negative version of the show.

Details – Interior space Table with a book stood up covered with a dustsheet, DSR (downstage right) corner, and 2 chairs mid stage a chair front and the one behind facing back also covered in dustsheet.

Exterior space – two tables one on either side of the set, each with a bottle and a glass.

Performers enter on either side, (preferably stage right) walk round one side of box looking at it, have a chat amongst themselves etc. and then walk behind the set out of view.

Sarah Enters SRD (stage right door) - Jake on roof - Sound change
Mole Enters SRD - Tim on roof

Jake and Tim look around the roof space and peer over the front to watch Marie and Sarah.

Mole Chalks an arrow on hatch No. 7 pointing down and an arrow on hatch 5 pointing up.

Marie Enters SLD (stage left door), Sarah leaves SLD. Marie sits down facing front, Sarah moves to the SL (stage left) proscenium arch, Mole moves around USR (upstage right) table, Marie leaves SLD, closing door, Mole sits down in her place with back to audience. Sarah watches from proscenium arch, Marie joins Sarah and whispers in Sarah's ear. Marie leaves and is followed by Sarah.

Marie Enters SLD, whispers in Mole's ear and leads him out.

Marie Returns through SLD, closing it, just as Jake posts a letter through hatch No. 5, which flutters, to the floor. She opens hatch 5, reaches up and is picked up by Tim and Jake. They disappear out of sight

Sarah Enters SLD, closing it, sees the letter on the floor and picks it up. She stands underneath hatch 7, opens letter and reads.

Within a social space such as a theatre, multiple and complex interactions are taking place, all of us performing in some sense, even in what we understand to be 'real life'. A performance thus extends beyond the deliberate artwork into its immediate social and physical environment. A performance might start in the bar or on the journey to the venue, at the moment the ticket is purchased, or when a person first hears about and anticipates it.

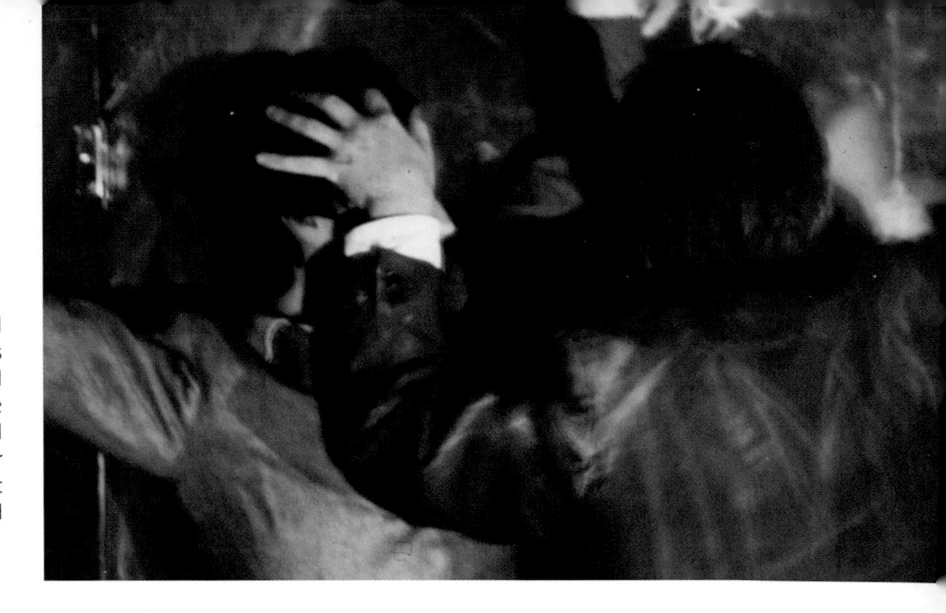

CHAPTER 5

OPENINGS

But I think we use personal maps a lot. not just in the presentations. in devising work or like when we constructed 'The Last Supper'. I asked everyone to write down the image of each scene. In a way this was a great exercise to ensure that we all had the same location. albeit imaginary.

Reckless Sleepers work with the notion of continuum in performance. Although typically witnessed between the hours of 8 and 9pm the notion that the performance is ongoing is explored long before the audience takes its seats. In 'Schrödinger's Box', the spaces stage right and stage left are extensions of the set and since there is no offstage performers must assume themselves visible at every point. Behind the scenes there is much unseen but equally focused activity, as when behind the doors and hatches the performers play a vital role in the proceedings within the set's interior.

Before a performance Mole will create a personal map of it in his head, placing images in a particular order. This has come about in response to a personal need to prepare, especially for new and unfamiliar performances. Sports psychologists have been using the same visualization technique for years.

As with classical physics, all actions and text have a cause (a history) and effect (what is witnessed). The time leading up to and including the opening of a performance sets the tone for the entire experience. In 'Spanish Train' the placing of a shoe outside the venue gives the impression that an event has already taken place, further reinforced by video footage seen on leaving the performance of Mole and Leen running from the train station. Mole mentions in his opening speech that 'we nearly didn't get here, the train was late and we had to run from the train station'.

At the formal start of 'Schrödinger's Box' objects within the set (a chair and a table) are first seen covered with dustsheets, as though in storage or transit. In the re-devising it was discussed whether the performance might open with a huge dustsheet spread over the entire set, with furniture and smaller objects within it covered by smaller sheets. The same fabric could later appear in the hands of the performers as handkerchiefs (also making reference to magicians). Playing with scale in such ways provides further visual metaphors for macro and micro worlds.

This covering and revealing also played a part in the museum project 'Creating the Past/Faraday's Cage'. The grand opening took the form of a procession featuring two large glass houses through the National Museum of Scotland. Each glass house was covered by flowing material that formed the trains of Grace Surman and Jess Hoffman's dresses.

I like the idea of opening or unwrapping a present as part of a theatrical event. In 'Three Wise Men' we wear 20 or so jumpers. Each time we take one off we make an entrance. an opening. A lot of the objects in 'Shakespeare Murders' are wrapped up or buried inside the Guy Fawkes dummies. These are smaller theatres with smaller curtains.

THE LETTER

We hear Mole in the background reading the text at the same time, there are subtle differences, but the timing is the same.

Sarah/Mole: And you appeared out of nowhere, as if you had come straight out of the ground and stood right in front of me looking harder and harder past me through me and away past me into some other time you looked angry and bitter or perhaps I wanted you to look that way. So I spent the day looking and laughing.
I couldn't speak; words had been shaken away, so I drank some more. And so much more that the room began to spin objects moved away from me I couldn't stop them they were out my control. So I stood in the middle of the room away from the walls waiting for your assistance.
Falling over again and again it was hot and then it was cold, I was waiting and waiting, to perhaps catch a glimpse of your proud face, standing upright turning and spinning me around your little finger,
I had to catch my breath I couldn't breathe without making and shaking a noise that said that I was near that I was tilted that my body needed to take in some more oxygen or alcohol I couldn't be sure.
You said that I had walked into the bedroom the red room as a doctor in a white coat and mask as I brought in a measured bottle a glass, a set of instructions a label for each object a mark for each time that I fell. I wanted to surrender to the charms of your spells your wicked concoctions, but your kisses were not the kisses I had grown used to.
When you called me I span when you whispered I turned, the smallest action produced an uneven reaction, so again I span and tumbled and fell into the rain.

Sarah moves back towards the SRD, as Sarah opens the door, we see Mole appear at the side of SR (stage right) proscenium arch, as she closes the door she continues to read out the rest of the letter but slowly fades out so that we can only hear Mole.

Mole/Sarah: You called me again and asked me to go upstairs I and I couldn't help thinking that I had been here before that somehow my time was being repeated in cycles .

Sarah fades out: in predictable cycles going over old ground travelling in circles.
But we always hit the same point a critical point in time.

And then it all stopped.

Sarah stops reading

Mole My time or your time was it my time to look inside to look at myself without a mirror, to list the very things that made sense to me and to list those things that I couldn't understand.

CHAPTER 6

LETTERS

You said that I had walked into the bedroom the red room. as a doctor in a white coat and mask as I brought in a measured bottle a glass, a set of instructions a label for each object, a ~~mark~~ mark for each time that I fell.

I wanted to surrender to the charms of your spells your wicked concoctions,

BUT YOUR KISSES WERE NOT THE KISSES I HAD GROWN USED TO

When you called me I ~~spam~~ span when you whispered I ~~fell~~ turned, the smallest action produced an uneven reaction, so again I span and tumbled and fell into the rain.

You called me again. and asked me to go upstairs and I couldn't help thinking that I had been here before that somehow my time was being repeated in cycles in predictable cycles going over old ground travelling in circles.

But we always hit the same point a critical point in time.

And then it all stopped.

My time or your time was it my time to look inside to look at myself without a mirror, to list the very things that made sense to me and to list those things I couldn't understand

Letters have great significance for me. it's the delay. and that the whole world changes in the 2–3 days it takes for them to arrive. I also write letters that are never to be sent. their intended recipient will not receive them. The letter in 'Schrödinger's Box' is two such letters bound together.

Letters are an illustration of how you feel right there and then. Even if you are in a bad mood at the beginning of a letter you are perhaps feeling better towards the end. One can also put down a letter and pick it up and continue writing it the following day. The reader. unless told. has no idea where and how this letter was written. This characteristic of letters is part of their charm. that details about them can be missing.

The letter in 'Schrödinger's Box' is not a love letter despite it being so called. It also wasn't sent. and its intention was never to be sent. It was written to someone I didn't see anymore. someone who existed and still does. but not in the same way. and to a future person who also is not a known. nor a given. in fact not at all.

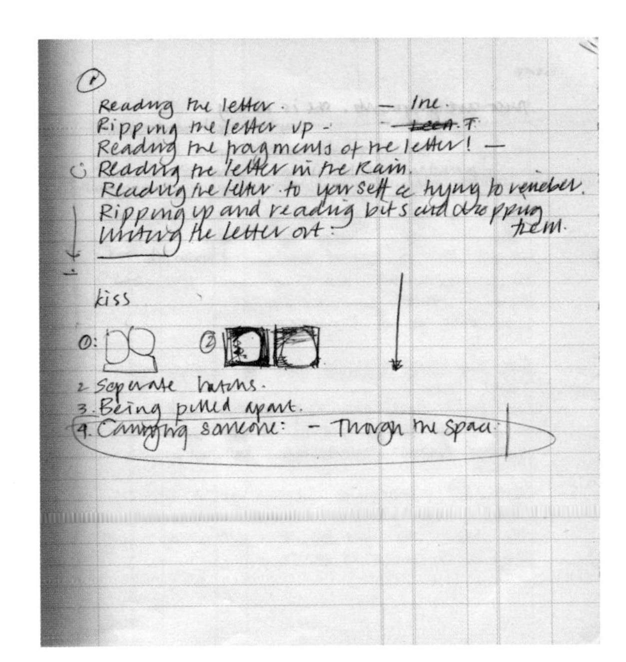

Reading the letter. — Ine.
Ripping the letter up - — T.
Reading the fragments of the letter! —
Reading the letter in the Rain.
Reading the letter to yourself & trying to remember.
Ripping up and reading bits and dropping them.
Writing the letter out:

kiss

2 Separate batons.
3. Being pulled apart.
4. Carrying someone: - Through the space.

In some of the initial research the company found letters that Einstein had written to his wife, a fellow scientist, in which he discussed relativity alongside the weather and expressions of his feelings towards her. Although this content is not referenced in 'Schrödinger's Box', the concept of time relativity is, being appropriate to the multiple viewpoints of Reckless Sleepers' theatre. A letter is the initial written text in the performance and is read aloud together by Mole and Sarah, from different parts of the space, suggesting long-distance correspondence and synchronous events.

The original text of the letter was written by Mole at 4am after waking from sleep. As a result a deliberate process was established of conducting certain tasks between 4 and 5am.

It was something I became aware of; having to get up early for a flight I remember my brain working in a very different way. It seemed quicker. funnier; like I was running and then I would just crash and fall asleep again. Some details are picked up while others are over people's heads. My mum for instance picked up on the Monroe and Chanel No.5/Marie Antoinette links in 'The Last Supper'. it is also the perfume she wore. and I think she found some link there.

The piece is semi biographical. in that I wrote it as my dad was dying. I think that there is always going to be some relationship to your own life. and experiences. that find their way into what you're making. My mum's last words are now in 'The Last Supper'. and form the basis for the improvised text that I say for Napoleon Bonaparte.

Leaving the UK I started to understand the complexities and beauty of the English language; it was like starting again. Also learning another language made me think about language in a different way. about the meanings of words. how we make connections with words and. for me. images. The act of writing the text also makes a great image. Advertising is something we use a lot in the work. my dad was a calligrapher and calligraphy. posters. banners and signs are an integral part of who I am.

Details and consistencies make satisfying connections between the multiple systems of a performance. A pack of Chesterfield cigarettes upon the table connects with James Dean, being the brand he used to smoke. The many pieces of rice paper eaten during the performance, each with text written on it, make reference to the scraps of paper upon which Franz Kafka wrote in his last moments when he was unable to speak. After the Geneva performance of 'The Last Supper' an audience member asked if Mole knew about Kafka's little pieces of paper.

This was a fantastic moment for me. not only because someone made an effort to come and ask me this question. the fact that they saw this detail and recognised its significance. I don't make it a huge statement and in no way do we isolate this fact. but even in its subtlety someone got it.

During the re-devising of 'Schrödinger's Box' Mole suggested that an investigation be made into the letter's journey, its reading, appearance and disappearance, and the different forms it might assume.

In one of a number of processes and tasks, Leen read the letter aloud in a different pattern, as though she was reading it for the first time (which she was), and breathed life into what was previously 'stuck'. She went on to cut it up, whereupon it became a snowstorm, a further instalment in the letter's journey. Finally she read the text aloud as written on each of the flakes of 'snow'. Some of these were blank.

Tim and Ine wrote out extracts on the walls in chalk and then read the text aloud as they walked around the space, forwards and backwards. They also performed involuntary cut ups of the letter as each read and then tried to recall the letter, aloud. It became apparent that not fully understanding the letter's content made it significantly harder to remember. What was remembered revealed what was most important to them. It was also interesting to observe each of them thinking, struggling to recall.

Tim:
I looked at you and you looked at me, and you were spinner err spinning around my little finger

And then I waited and it was hard and I was expecting something from you but I couldn't remember what and we were spinning again and then ooooh you looked through me harder and harder past me away from me away past me

Mole:
I had to catch my breath I couldn't breathe...without making or shaking a noise you said that I was near

Some more ol..alcohol I couldn't be sure, or oxygen I couldn't be sure, you said that we had walked into the bedroom the redroom in a white coat and mask my body was tilted I was shaking.

Lists
As you brought in a bottle a glass

And then it all stopped my time or your time

Leen:
You said ... something

erm.. I was.. I was.. in the bedroom or the redroom as the Doctor said.....

erm......some measurements...a glass

and

then it all stopped

My time or your time

I didn't know , I didn't know

and the kisses were not the kisses I was used to

Time in cycles....comes back

and it was.....(can't hear properly)

Mole has always created storyboards for Reckless Sleepers' performances, involving visual texts or graphic sets of instructions, with simple sketches i.e. a person, moving in a particular direction, carrying a basket. Early storyboards enabled things to be processed further, such as interpreting movement from graphic marks. Such notation is not concerned with fixing as in Labanetics, for example, but reflects the adaptive nature of Reckless Sleepers' theatre.

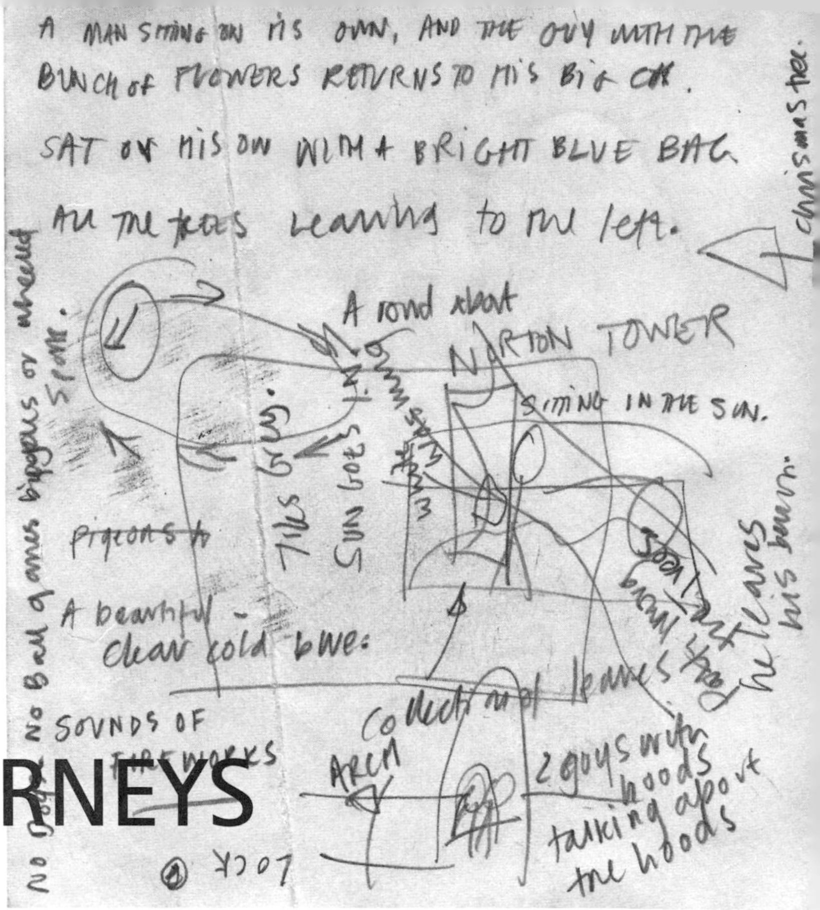

We started really pushing maps. marks in 'In the Shadow'. It seems that now this has become part of our repertoire.

CHAPTER 7

MAPS AND JOURNEYS

Memory maps, in which a performance is visualised, are routinely used.

A process called 'Intentions' is used in which each presents a cue, logic or intention of his or her performance. 'Intentions' is a means of drawing out or exposing the internal logics of a performer's journey and also ensures that fellow performers understand that they are not only needed for cues but sometimes function as an element in another's internal logic.

In 'Parasite' this was born of a need, as the piece had a complex structure and action was taking place both inside and outside. 'Intentions' must be done both as a group as well as individually as Mole needs to know what is going on inside each person's head.

I love this process. We did a run through version of 'Schrödinger's Box' in a flat in Edinburgh. we knew the piece and wanted to make it fun again. play with it and entertain each other.

In 'The Last Supper' I stand up as Napoleon Bonaparte. I have an image of him standing with his back to us. looking out to sea. It's windy. This image is joined by another of him in bed. shouting out nonsense. I have images for all parts of the performance. and sometimes these images are very detailed. each time I do this performance the images grow.

Much of the text in Reckless Sleepers' work paints imaginary worlds. Although the performers in 'The Last Supper' rely upon cue points as well as memory maps, a similar process was used in which everyone was asked to articulate the image evoked in relation to a particular personality in the performance.

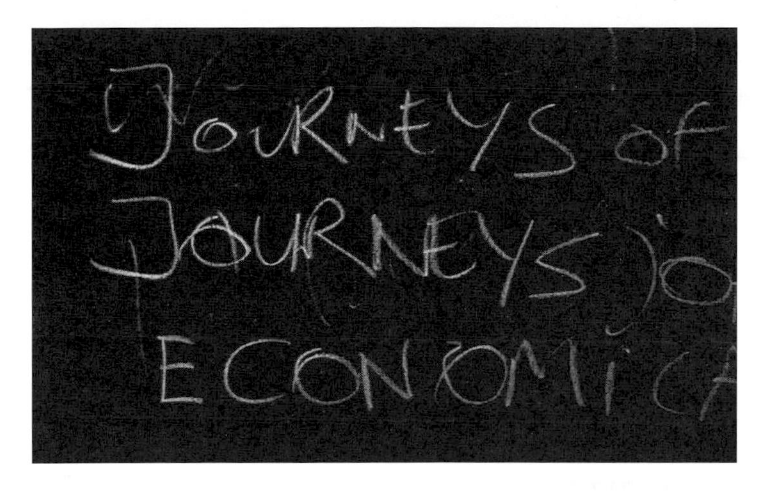

The letter is a constant throughout the piece but in the process of looking again I wanted to expand its presence. the journey that it might take through the performance. or the transformation that it could go through. So we see it being ripped up and then later we see it as a snowstorm. This process of pushing an object. or a moment. is key in the making process. We also see it in the drinking scene where Tim tries to maintain order. I think what I am interested in now is how much more we can get out of the letter. where else it fits.

I always see Marilyn Monroe in a hotel bed a lot of sheets a bed with a bright light. wood on 1960s bedside cabinets. which is very clear to me. It's hard to shift this image.

This image also makes me listen. and I have the impression that this is what we are doing with 'The Last Supper'. we are making images. with the words that we use.

Reckless Sleepers has an abiding interest in journeys, be it of an idea, a particular performer or object through a performance. Each has its own opening, the start of its journey through the performance, as well as a life before and after. Human intervention takes the set and the objects within it, such as the letter, on their respective journeys.

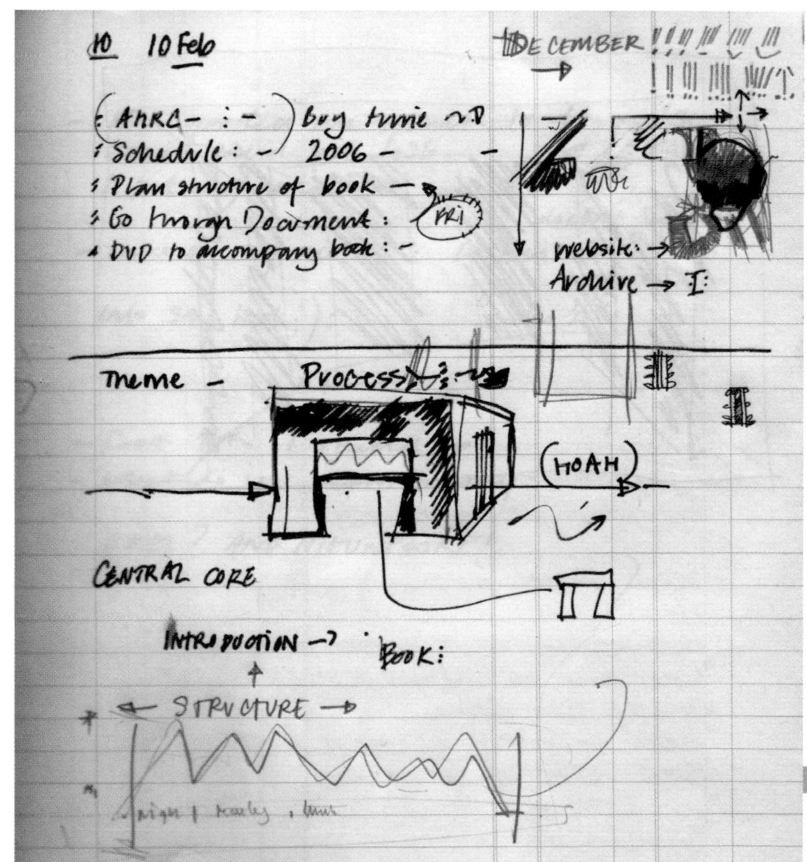

The letter, in common with all other objects, has a series of four different scenes, four states based upon a structure that creates relationships between elements. The letter's journey involves transformation, from paper into snow. This might not necessarily be in the conventional sequence, in reference to time relativity.

I chose the number 4 randomly. it could have been 5 but I was interested in the four elements. Fire. Water. Earth and Air as a way of honing down and then pushing new scenes from each element. For instance Tim believes there is a fire in the room so I would like there to be three further fire references in the piece. It's a mathematical thing. but a key means of structuring pieces. It also means that we don't just stick to one idea or the first thing. we have to invent three more scenes

Trains are a recurring motif in Reckless Sleepers' work. Their relevance to 'Schrödinger's Box' lies in Einstein's description of two trains to express relativity in one of his thought experiments. Trains are also present in the paintings of both de Chirico and Magritte. Much of Mole's writing for Reckless Sleepers has been done whilst travelling on trains or waiting at train stations. This accords with the experience of other artists such as Graeme Miller (Watt, J in Bannerman, C (ed) 2006, p.193) who has described taking 'gratuitous train journeys' that allow space for thought.

I made a conscious effort to write something every time I was on a journey. It was a very deliberate process. 'A House on a Hill' one of the 'this is...' texts in 'Schrödinger's Box'. was written on journeys to and from Belgium.

Something I would still like to do is to take a train journey to Madrid. to pay homage. to do some writing. take some photographs or film. I want to explore the other possibilities in 'Spanish Train'. I really need to look at everything that we can do with this one project.

The expansion of singular ideas is evident in other projects. 'In the Shadow' made much use of maps. in the form of pieces of card with diagrams and other instructions that became 'Breaking Symmetry'. derived from 'Schrödinger's Box'. 'House on a Hill' (2002). was based upon the 'This is...' scene.

The construction of maps was/is used as one of the bases for 'Quiet Time'. in which a 10-minute walk became an observational experience. Maps constituted a large part of this residency programme and the processes that developed from it. 'Quiet Time' walking processes were used in the nighttime walks in 'Sleepers'.

This is a long train journey

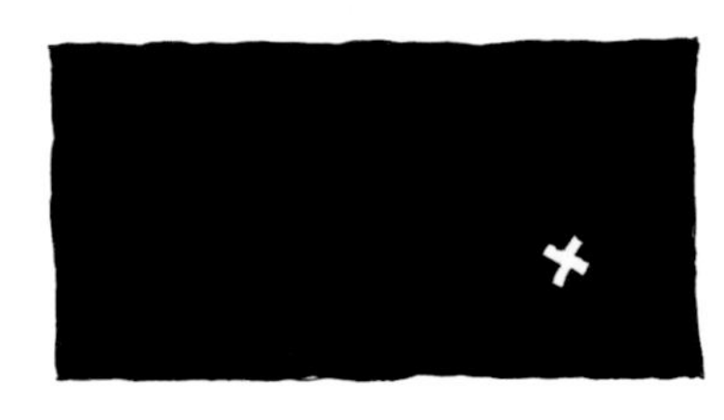

This is hard

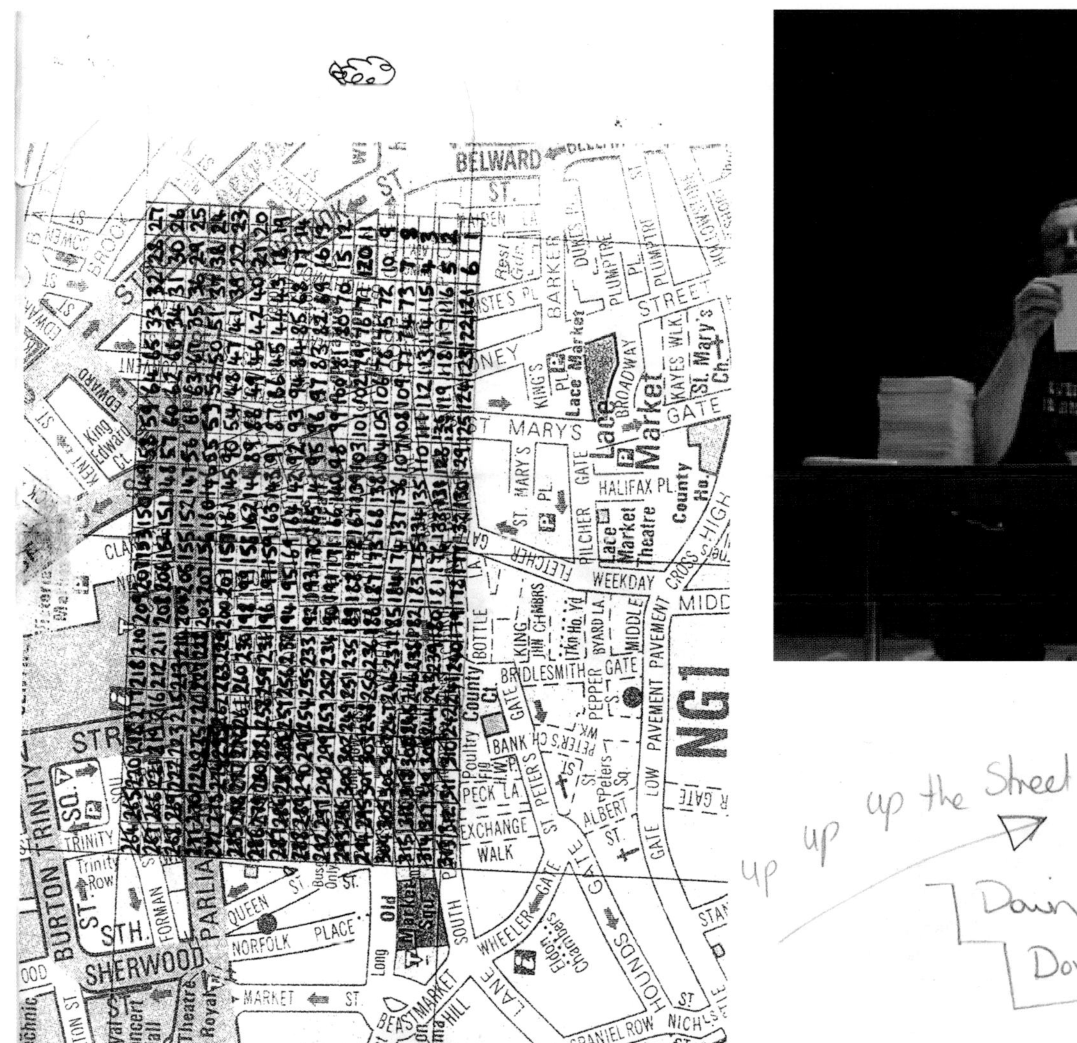

In 'The Last Supper' we spent a lot of time researching and inventing last words and last scenarios. We also played a game called 'Botticelli' in which one person says the name of someone. say 'Napoleon Bonaparte'. The following person (clockwise) has to come up with a famous person whose first name begins with the first letter of the surname of the previous person in this case B and could say 'Bruce Springsteen'. The next would have to start with an S say 'Shirley Bassey'. The following person has to start with a B first name and if they chose someone with a first and last name the same say 'Brigitte Bardot'. then the direction would change to anticlockwise.

NUMBERS

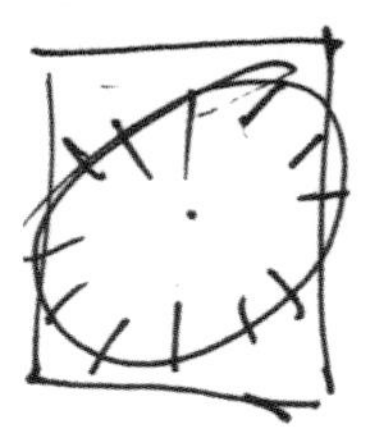

Jake falls through ceiling hatch 7. Everyone looks through the nearest hatch and looks at Jake and then close their hatch.

Mole moves round to SR proscenium arch.

Marie enters SLD with some cards, draws around Jake and sits down.

Marie shows the audience her cards.

Marie: Number 1 (drops card)

Mole draws a clock on SR proscenium arch

Marie: Number 2 (drops card)

Mole draws an arrow and underneath a figure falling.

Sarah enters SRD leading Tim by the hand. She places him in USL (upstage left) corner with his arms outstretched holding on to the corners of the nearest hatches.

Mole leaves proscenium arch and goes behind set

Sarah moves to the open SRD and chalks a No. 3 on the hatch.

Mole opens hatch in SLD (a No. 3 is revealed on it) puts a hammer through.

Tim averts his eyes, and Mole drops the hammer.

Marie picks up the hammer.

Tim looks scared and backs away along the USC (upstage centre) wall.

Marie opens ceiling hatch 3 with the hammer and then draws around it onto the open hatch door.

Tim removes dustsheet from table DSR, revealing a book, opens DSR hatch and throws sheet through and starts to read book facing the audience.

Mole opens hatch in SRD and gives Sarah a glass of water, which she throws over Jake

Jake is still on the floor.

Marie leaves by SLD closing it.

Mole gives Sarah another glass of water to throw over Jake and then she leaves SRD closing it.

Jake stands up, removes jacket and places it over the spilt water. He walks towards the table before Tim (takes the drinking pose No.3), turns book so that he can read it, climbs on to the table, turns around and exits backwards through open DSR hatch taking table and book with him, closing hatch. Tim stands there looking confused.

As Jake exits, Marie enters SLD, with an identical table and book and places it under hatch 5 and reads the book. Tim sits down behind this table, Marie leaves through SLD, closing it, as Mole enters through SRD with cards and dustsheet. He closes the book, whispers to Tim – who nods – places cards on table in front of Tim and covers Tim's head with the sheet and exits SRD closing it. During this, Sarah appears in proscenium arch SL bottom hatch eating an apple; Marie appears in opposite hatch and places apple outside, closing hatch. Tim is observed through various hatches.

drawing at start

BACKGROUND LAYER:
SOUND:

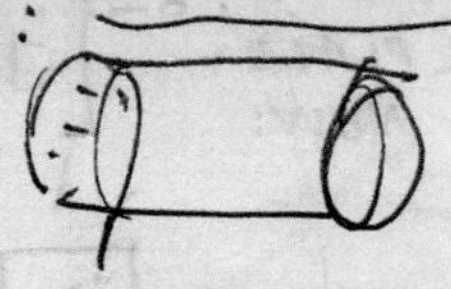

COLLECTING SOME RECORDS / EVENTS OF CRASHES -
WHERE THEY TAKE PLACE:

WHY WE TRAVEL - WHY DO WE TAKE JOURNEYS -

WHAT DO WE DO WHEN WE GET SOMEWHERE.

- UNSCHEDULED STOPS -

(MOTORWAYS)
- BASICALLY A FORWARD MOVEMENT →

→ APART FROM IN TOWNS -

quite a big section
'this movement has no meaning which way will they go?
Text (1)

WHAT THINGS ARE MADE OF & WHAT HAPPENS TO THIS MATERIAL:

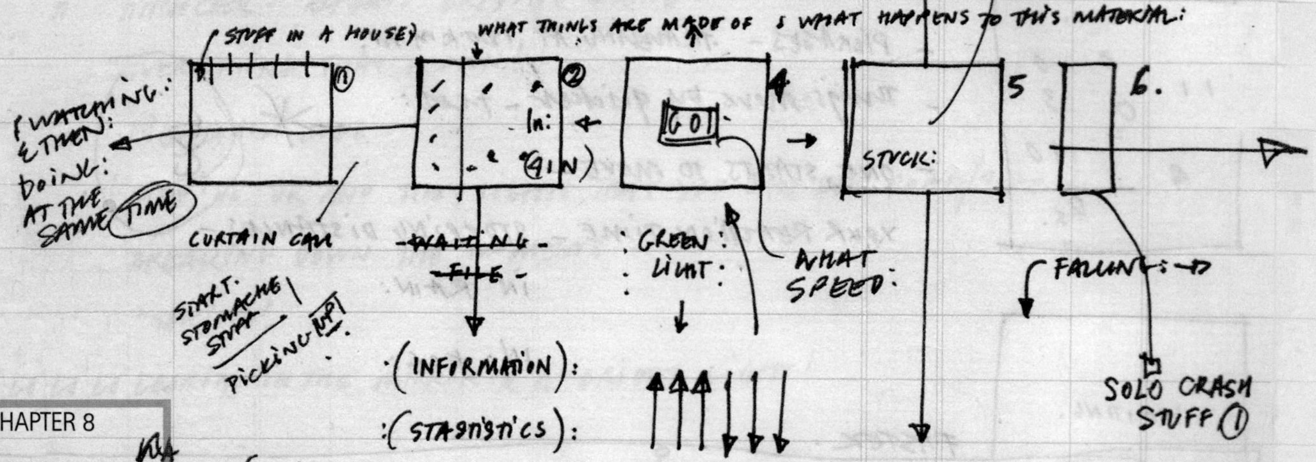

(STUFF IN A HOUSE) (1) (2) 4 5 6.

WATCHING & THEN: DOING: AT THE SAME TIME

CURTAIN CALL

in: (GIN)

GO!

STUCK:

~~WAITING~~ - ~~FILE~~ -

GREEN LIGHT:

WHAT SPEED:

FALLING: →

START. STOMACHE STRAP / PICKING UP!

:(INFORMATION):

:(STATISTICS):

SOLO CRASH STUFF (1)

CHAPTER 8

MIDDLES

STOPPING:

MOVEMENT WITHOUT MEANING!

WITH TEXT - SOME - TRAVEL EXERCISES -

DESTINATION TEXT!

~~KORTRIJK~~ - ~~BARCELONA~~ - TRAVEL TIME -

KORTRIJK - LILLE - TRAVEL TIME - 1hr 20 mins - BLACKSPOTS - -

- DANGEROUS BITS -

EATHQUAKE = BODY TREMOR - SHIVERING SHOCK

- NO - APPARENT DANGER -

WANDERING [LOST] LIKE IN MULHOLAND DRIVE!

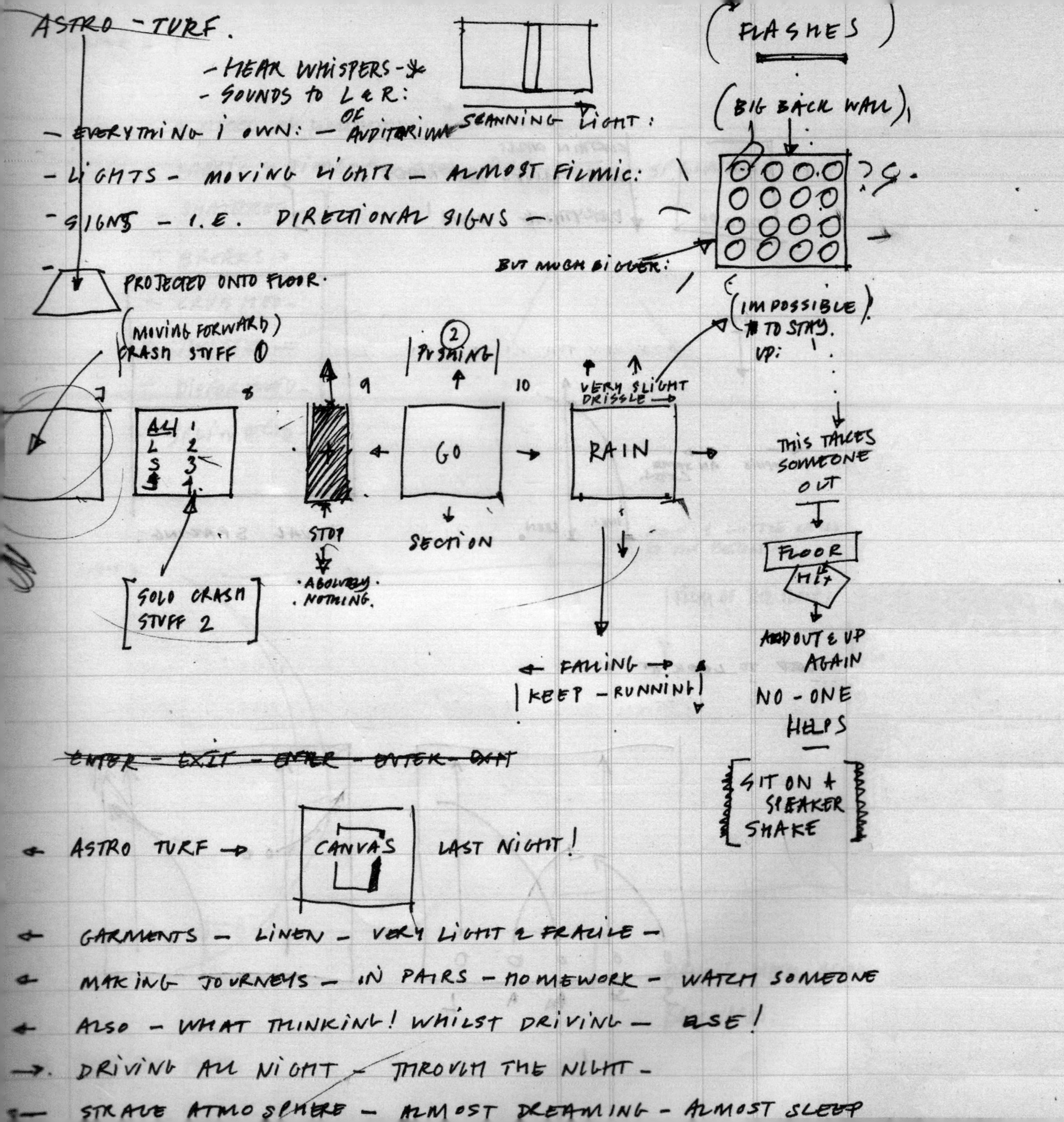
ASTRO - TURF.
- HEAR WHISPERS -
- SOUNDS TO L & R: OF AUDITORIUM
- EVERYTHING I OWN: -
SCANNING LIGHT:
(FLASHES)
(BIG BACK WALL)
- LIGHTS - MOVING LIGHTS - ALMOST FILMIC:
- SIGNS - I.E. DIRECTIONAL SIGNS -
BUT MUCH BIGGER:
PROJECTED ONTO FLOOR.
(MOVING FORWARD)
CRASH STUFF 1
(IMPOSSIBLE TO STAY UP:
2
PUSHING
7
8
9
10
VERY SLIGHT DRISSLE
ALL 1
L 2
S 3
4
GO
RAIN
STOP
ABSOLUTELY NOTHING.
SECTION
THIS TAKES SOMEONE OUT
FLOOR
HIT
AND OUT & UP AGAIN
SOLO CRASH STUFF 2
FALLING
KEEP - RUNNING
NO - ONE HELPS
ENTER - EXIT - ENTER - ENTER - EXIT
SIT ON A SPEAKER SHAKE
ASTRO TURF
CANVAS
LAST NIGHT!
GARMENTS - LINEN - VERY LIGHT & FRAGILE -
MAKING JOURNEYS - IN PAIRS - HOMEWORK - WATCH SOMEONE
ALSO - WHAT THINKING! WHILST DRIVING - ELSE!
DRIVING ALL NIGHT - THROUGH THE NIGHT -
STRANGE ATMOSPHERE - ALMOST DREAMING - ALMOST SLEEP

To get to the middle you have come from somewhere. In the middle of the performance. you are there and then heading towards the end. It's a simple trinity; beginning. middle and end.

Structuring. setting up dynamics. transitions where things crossover. the architecture of a piece and how the experience of it is managed. We see a new structure like a Molecular model. i.e. Mole = n atoms.

I think that the structures are where I feel most comfortable. putting something together on paper. its a really satisfying moment. like the writing of 'The Last Supper'. all that information and research pared down into a one hour performance. The process of structuring is mostly cutting things away and paring them down in order to build them up again.

Starting with an idea pushing it away from the source. but we always come back to the beginning again. Working on this process has been strange because all that information is stored in a place in my head. and it has come alive again.

This bit when the pieces are crafted and put together is the most enjoyable of the making of a performance. Historically what we have normally got is a collection of fragments and scenes. like jigsaw puzzle pieces on the floor. We pick them up and place them on the table. Each performance has its own strategy for the way things are put together.

'Schrödinger's Box' was structured as though events took place over the course of a day. morning. afternoon. evening and night. The structures for the early work

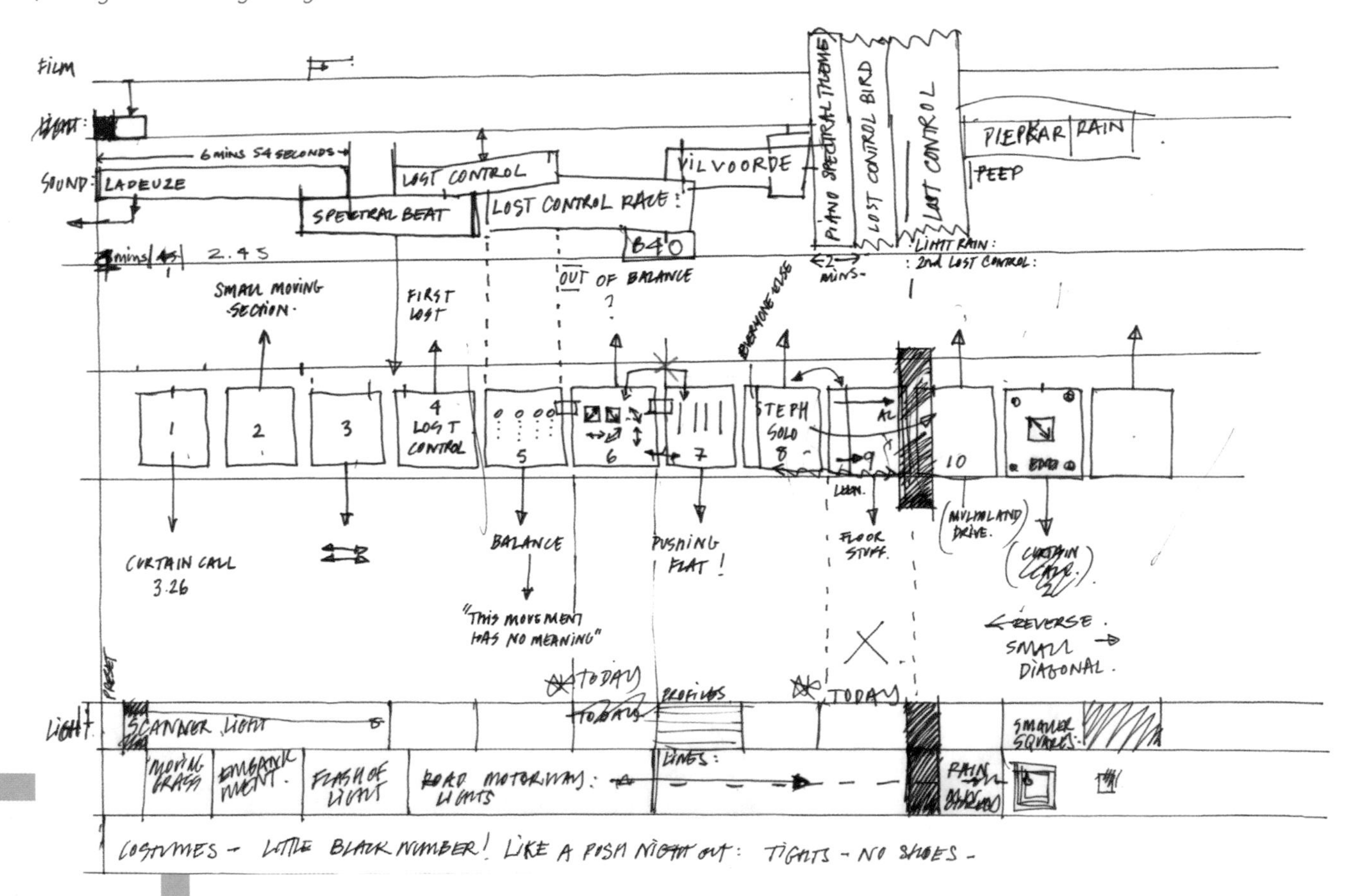

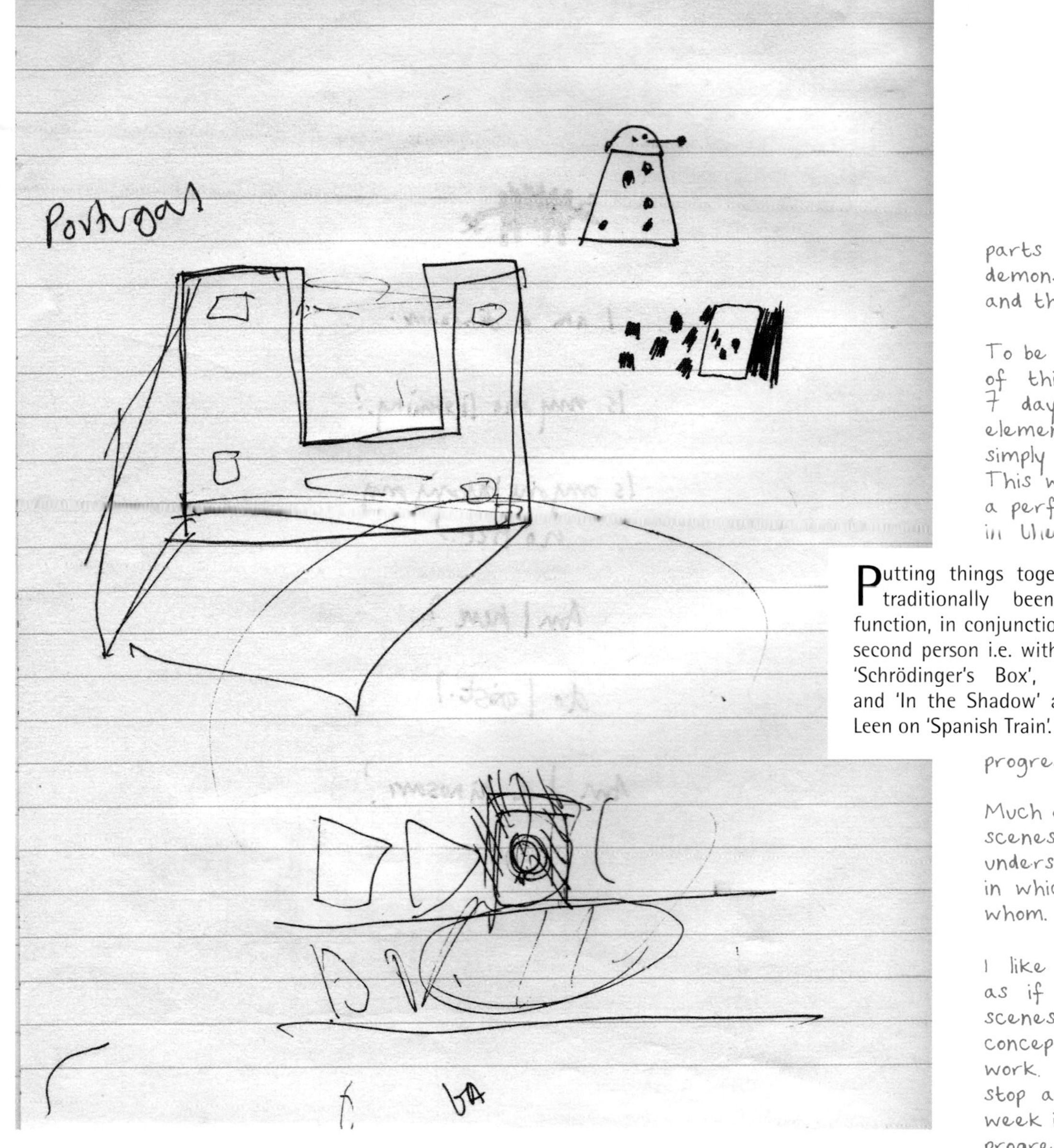

were originally in storyboard form. Now a single piece of paper is used, with small drawings and text representing scenes, and arrows showing movement. This is normally a single sheet, or I use a double page in my notebook.

Each scene is within a little square and all that takes place happens around the edges. If you had to remake a piece you would require this document, the closest thing to a score. It is useful to show to everyone else in this format. The process of articulation then reveals parts that require rewriting. It demonstrates the whole, the holes and the links.

To be most efficient the rehearsal of this structure would be done 7 days before a premiere, the elements already existing and simply being ordered near the end. This would allow enough time if as a performer you had been involved in the devising of the work. But some artists want to know much earlier, making clear distinctions between different phases: research, devising, rehearsing, rewriting, work in progress, and final rehearsals.

Putting things together has traditionally been Mole's function, in conjunction with a second person i.e. with Dan on 'Schrödinger's Box', 'Parasite' and 'In the Shadow' and with Leen on 'Spanish Train'.

Much of devising isn't about making scenes, it's about creating an understanding of this new world in which we operate, the rules, of whom, how and why.

I like playing with material, it's as if I can't stop creating new scenes and new ideas that fit the conceptual structure of a piece of work. However the process must stop at some point, usually in the week immediately before a work in progress presentation, which imposes a deadline. The work in progress acts as a focus, from which we get feedback from others, as well as recording and reviewing it on video ourselves. At this point we are still able to move away from it. A final week or more is then spent on 'finishing' the piece.

One can even set up quite ridiculous cases. A cat is penned up in a steel chamber, along with the following device (which must be secured against direct interference by the cat): in a Geiger counter there is a tiny bit of radioactive substance, so small, that perhaps in the course of the hour one of the atoms decays, but also, with equal probability, perhaps none; if it happens, the counter tube discharges and through a relay releases a hammer which shatters a small flask of hydrocyanic acid. If one has left this entire system to itself for an hour, one would say that the cat still lives if meanwhile no atom has decayed. The psi-function of the entire system would express this by having in it the living and dead cat (pardon the expression) mixed or smeared out in equal parts.
(Schrödinger, E., 1935)

CHAPTER 9

PHYSICS

Reckless Sleepers' proposition of 'Schrödinger's Box' makes it seem a playful space despite all the struggles that are apparently faced within. Childlike scientists conduct experiments on virtual cats, much as cats play with mice.

The origins of the set came about through playing with the idea of a 'scientists' retreat' which, if they had such a thing, might be somewhere to drink a cup of tea, compare notes, perform experiments and write equations using blackboards and chalk. The set or the box is many things, for each person it has a different sense of place. Marie and Jake's texts are attempts to illustrate this i.e. 'it is an observation chamber'.

'Schrödinger's Box' is firmly based upon observation; what takes place within is observable from the auditorium by means of the box's missing fourth wall. The performers view one another via the front and the multiple hatches. The roles of observer and observed are interchangeable.

The characters speak aloud, at times with or without the written text in their hands. The authorship of these texts is in doubt, some sound like they (or parts of them) have been borrowed from other, possibly scientific, sources. They enlighten or mystify in equal measure and influence the people, objects and action within the box. Truth and untruth (objective and subjective) are (truly) at the heart of the piece.

The walls, blank at the outset, are ultimately covered in a confusion of text and image, bewildering with potential interpretations and thus providing absolutely none. This provides a typically postmodern theatrical experience, in which the initiative for interpretation lays entirely with those who witness it.

As early as 1905 Albert Einstein announced his formulation of Special Relativity, a theory that shook classical science to its foundations, but makes particular sense in relation to theatre, and postmodern thought.

Events on two distant stars may appear simultaneous to one observer but successive to a differently situated observer (Marshall, I and Zohar, D 1997, p.319).

This is key and relates so well to the kind of work I want to make. dealing with space and time in theatre.

How do you explain the big bang? Is it someone dropping a cup? A lot of different theories are kicking about and can be illustrated in the theatre in a very interesting way.

I stumbled into Quantum Physics. I thank Dan for introducing this world to me. It's now very much a part of who I am.

The story or image that often fills my head is of a scientist with a cup and saucer. I'd imagine Alan Turing walking out in the dead of night, wearing a dressing gown and working something out, throwing the cup into the lake at the bottom of the garden.

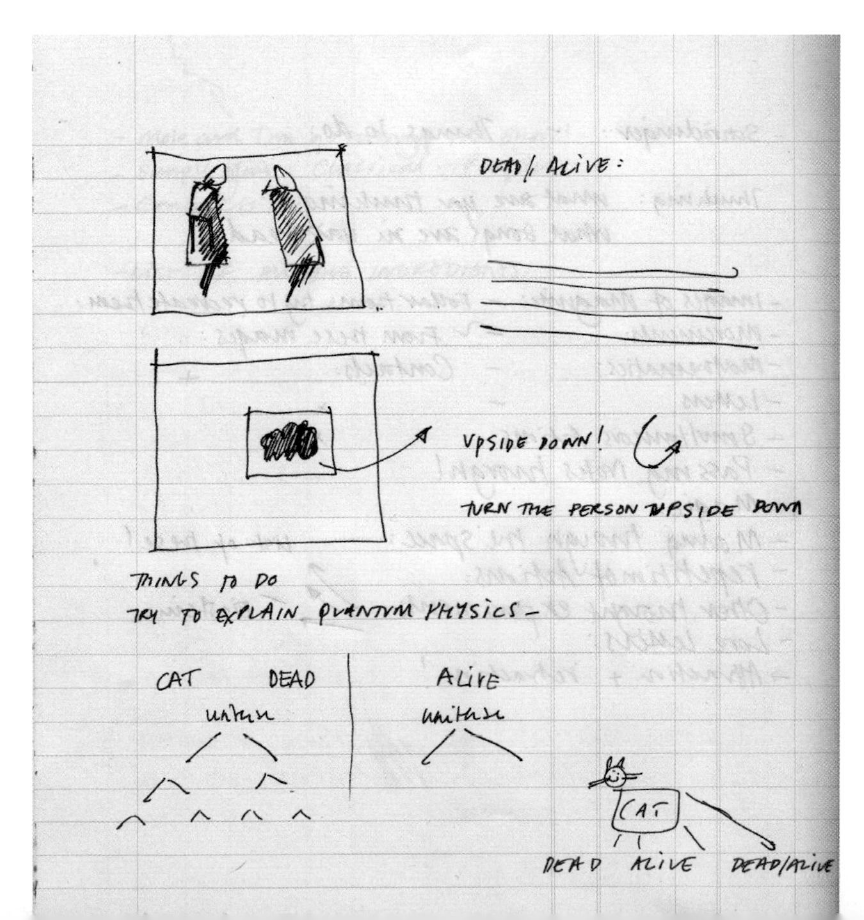

The 1920s saw breakthroughs in the field of Quantum Mechanics alongside related and similarly radical developments in the arts including the incorporation of chance, and multiple/non-linear narratives. The repercussions of Werner Heisenberg's Uncertainty Principle formulated in 1927 have been felt in many fields, not least in relation to the indeterminacy of much mid to late 20th century art.

The 1927 Solvay conference held in Brussels was attended by the key players in the 'new science'. A photograph of the event is reminiscent of Surrealist group photographs.

Although it ought to be possible to accommodate thinking that readily connects with the postmodern paradigm, the concepts behind Quantum Mechanics seem less acceptable than the straightforward irrationality to be found in much 20th Century discourse.

Quantum Theory and postmodernism place the existing perceptions of Newtonian physics and modernism within broader contexts. To minds brought up with and maintaining a firm grip upon the determinist model, Quantum Theory is closer to magic than science, the scientists 'performing it' resembling latter day magicians. In 'Schrödinger's Box' the division between magicians and scientists has been deliberately blurred, each having the capacity to deceive, literally pulling the rug out from under people's feet.
Magic is one of many layers in 'Schrödinger's Box'.

Classical science is taken for granted, and it's something that we can easily articulate and demonstrate. Quantum is different, but if we had knowledge of it earlier, younger then perhaps the ideas would be easy to understand. We don't really take Quantum Physics for granted, like we do evolution or gravity.

A bunch of flowers is presented with a flourish, legs appear through hatches, a woman is sawn in half (half alive/half dead - what have we done?), we witness various woman/cat superpositions. The 'this is...' scene resembles a mind-reading act where objects are wrongly identified. In Gent 'this is...' became 'I see...' alluding to magic acts and crystal gazing, another world, another form of escape, within the mind.

In 'Schrödinger's Box' the performers responsibly (or irresponsibly) make no attempt to explain the theories behind classical and quantum physics. But references to philosophy and practical physics have continued in Reckless Sleepers' works such as 'Breaking Symmetry' (1999), 'In the Shadow (2000) and 'The Turing Test' (2001).

Some key elements of Quantum Theory as well as classical physics, have found their way into processes and outcomes:

Heisenberg's Uncertainty Principle

Werner Heisenberg sought and found inspiration for his speculations into Quantum Mechanics by walking in the mountains. 'Schrödinger's Box' references both Heisenberg and his Uncertainty Principle. The thrust of the latter is that physical reality cannot be fully known because one's approach towards a phenomenon must exclude other complimentary, but legitimate, approaches. These might be in relation to the measurement of position and momentum, or by extension between structure and innovation, detailed observation and the big picture, or facts and the 'feel' of something. The Uncertainty Principle can be applied to the complimentary analytical and poetic ways in which Reckless Sleepers chooses to work. 'Both/and' thought is both possible and necessary in relation to Quantum Theory.

Superpositions

Quantum entities can experience more than one reality at a time, Schrödinger's wave function containing a plethora of possibilities, all equally real (and contradictory). White light is a superposition of all colours, space is filled with superposed radio and TV signals. For Reckless Sleepers this takes the form of 'Simultaneous Actions', a process in which actions, despite having the same intention, take very different forms.

Relativity

Relativity is deeply embedded in 20th Century thinking and underpins postmodern philosophy and the rejection of objective standards and fixed viewpoints. Relativity reveals our own notions of culture to be no more nor less subjective and valid as anyone else's. A fascination with relativity is manifest in the playing with time that takes place in 'Schrödinger's Box' and the ghosts of events and objects that inhabit the set of 'In the Shadow'.

A lot of times I ask someone to watch something and then to represent it. but not at the same time. there are gaps in time between observing and presenting. Therefore a lot of new things happen. you edit. forget things. and make things you like bigger than they actually were.

The originator is then able to see a facsimile or version of what they have done and subsequently make changes and develop. This is a subtle way of directing without directing.

The opportunity must be given to see things (8 times) before they sink in. I think seeing something over again reveals its potential. It's also something that makes you laugh. cry or feel uneasy.

I use repetition a lot in making work. Asking someone to watch a performance improvisation and to then show this to the maker. With this simple process new things are exposed. It is not really copying. it's processing an action or a scene. As a director I need to feel what an action is. as well as looking at it. In the drinking scene there are 4 numbers. each with a corresponding action. One of the numbers doesn't have an action so we don't know what to do.

Watching the drinking scene it is possible to see differences in the interpretation of this task. Sarah is always a little later than the other three and for me it is vital that each of us is different. each with our own way of moving and response time. We are. after all. human beings.

Different people in parallel spaces can perform the same action simultaneously. perhaps inside and outside the box. This device acts as choreographic glue that sticks things together. not in the sense of a 'chorus' or in mirroring. but in relation to the practical issue of sightlines. Because of the physical arrangement of the set it is possible to see left or right very clearly but not both. An action could take place on either side of the set and those sat in the middle may not see it at all.

We play a lot with sightlines. what you can and can't see. I like these divides that are so apparent in 'Parasite' and don't exist at all in 'Spanish Train'. Each person will witness a different performance because of where they chose or were directed to sit. In 'The Last Supper' this is a random process with strong consequences. as people choose their seats via a lottery and are generally separated from their friends. lovers and family. Most come in pairs and because they are broken up they are unable to maintain that strong unit that can stand apart from the social gathering. What takes place is that strangers sit next to. and talk to. one another. Once the performance is finished the food is normally shared. people tend to congregate around the two larger meals. The birthday cake holds a special position within the piece. even when it has ended.

one of us had an idea that the interior space was a multiple of spaces occupied not only by different forces but also different times. and having different functions i.e. a living room with tables and chairs. a grandfather clock or a grandmother clock. other 'time pieces'. a fireplace and pictures or photographs on the wall. A ghost would occupy this room and use these objects as if they were still present. even though both ghost and objects are not. 'Describing rooms' is a process that has often been used in Reckless Sleepers' projects ('In the Shadow'. 'Somewhere between Falling and Flying') and workshops. describing a familiar place in an unfamiliar setting. such as a theatre or a studio space.

I like to play with time in the construction of pieces. it's knowing that we have an hour of a person's time and within that hour I want them to have an experience that will somehow change them. I am conscious that we can return to an idea. it might make more sense at the end. We play most obviously with time and non-linear structure in 'Spanish Train' in which acts and parts are cut up and switched. part 1 skipping to part 3 and then into act 4. After the performance has finished we show the film of us running to the venue but it is obviously fake. for the most part it's dark outside when we were supposed to be running from the train station. but then we play with that a lot. with time. truths. and where we really are i.e. in a theatre sat next to a friend.

I think that timepieces (clocks) have a special significance for me. My grandfather. as well as working in a grocery shop. was a watch and clock repairer. (He fixed radios and motorbikes too). But he was mostly known for fixing clocks and watches. In his house there were hundreds of old clocks each set to a slightly different time. So 12 o'clock could last up to twenty minutes as chimes went off from 'ten to' to 'ten past' the hour.

Falling and catching are common themes in Reckless Sleepers' work, falling in love, falling down, references to real physical forces like gravity, as well as emotional forces.

From a standing position, Leen is asked to fall, not remaining in the same spot but allowing herself to travel across the space. As she sways, further and further from her centre (as though subject to forces beyond herself) she generates considerable tension among observers who feel as though they must rush to stop her. When, at last, she does go, it is backwards, into empty space. Tim steps across and gently stops her. While resembling a failed levitation act, this is a further device used for creating tension and generating emotion.

The arrow drawn pointing down on the hatch in 'Schrödinger's Box', seems to predict Jake's subsequent fall. His repeated falling, too, suggests a continuum, calling into question the chronology and status of the events that take place around his falling.

Gravity

As classical physics is accommodated within the paradigm of the Quantum, it likewise plays its part within the on and off stage worlds in which Reckless Sleepers operates. Apples and Jake falling are but two examples of the physical forces at play in both worlds.

Although technology could provide an illusion of freedom from gravitational forces the 'wires remain visible' and such endeavours might not anyway be particularly rewarding. More in keeping with the company's aesthetic is to play with gravity by throwing apples up through the ceiling hatches and wait an unnaturally long time for them to return. The length of wait is critical, the thrower remaining in position until the apple falls, at which point they are invariably caught unawares. This relates to 'Passive/Active' (for explanation refer to page 75). Expectations can be further tested by a person who is holding an apple aloft themselves being pulled up through a hatch.

Gravity exists. we cannot defy it but we have force at our disposal that is greater. thus we are able to fly

Another process involves a person sat at a table on which a row of apples is placed. The table is set at an increasing angle, and tension mounts as the apples approach their tipping point. Finally friction no longer holds them in place and they tumble to the floor. In a related activity Ine and Leen behave as though the box is being steadily tilted. When it seems they can go no further Tim enters and falls in the opposite direction.

The artists experiment with falling. Tim throws a 'faint' and ends up in a fallen position but with his legs in the air, as though time have been frozen.

It is as if we identify these forces and ultimately contradict them.

One of my favourite moments in the history of 'Schrödinger's Box' is captured on video, from a performance at the Green Room in Manchester. As we used wine glasses made from real glass there were frequent breakages, especially in the drinking scene. Thus we introduced a system where Tim would shout 'STOP', (a real response) and then enter the space with a dustpan and brush to clear up the glass. The video recording shows him cleaning up and, as he leaves, slipping and falling, which always makes me laugh. It's an incredible fall; we noticed that his legs stay up, off the ground. We could never reproduce this moment because it will only happen once. It is predictable that a breakage may happen again, and Tim may fall again, but the chances of this happening are remote, and I wouldn't like to push it. What's significant here is the sudden break into REALITY that exists outside the piece. It's an unpredictability of an event that might happen and we have inserted a strategy to deal with it. I know that if it ever happened again I would probably have to contain my laughter, not for what I was seeing but more about the memory of what happened in Manchester.

Both these examples of falling are repeated. Tim's awkward fall has a clumsy quality, whereas Ine's is more of a dancer's fall, being fluid. I would look at ways of making this awkward, difficult, clumsy, even ugly.

Ine is instructed to fall when a word starting with a letter between A to H is spoken. She repeats this fall, again and again and again.

THIS IS (RORSCHACH CARDS)

Tim (blindfolded) picks up the cards one at a time showing the image to the audience.
Guessing what is drawn on them, he shows the cards upside down, and so therefore he is not reading them right.

Tim: This is a teacup
This is a briefcase
This is a blackboard
This is a filing cabinet
This is an egg...frying

Sarah leaves apple core outside proscenium arch and closes hatch. Mole appears at SL proscenium arch; Marie stands before SR proscenium arch and draws an apple and a wine glass, crossing out Mole's drawings. Mole picks up the apple and pockets it.

Tim This is a lake in Switzerland
This is an apple

Mole takes an apple from his other pocket and puts it on floor. They both leave.

Tim: This is a cheese sandwich
This is a picket fence

Mole enters SLD stands by Tim, hits Tim over the head, turns the cards the right way up he whispers instructions to Tim and leaves SLD, closing it.
Marie appears at SL proscenium arch,
pockets apple and watches Tim

Tim: This is a moustache
This is a hat stand (turns card 90 degrees)
This is a dead cat rotting
This is a field of wheat in summer

Marie: It's an experimental chamber...

Tim: This is a tree on a hill in Belgium

Marie: ...a cloud chamber...

Tim: This is ice melting

Marie: ...a crucible, a radio, a tuning device.

Tim: This is a nose

Marie: It is so blank it can call other rooms in to being.

Tim: This...reminds me of something

Marie: It's a psychological test to see what you can create in the blankness

Tim: This is a woman I haven't met yet
It's about time

Marie: It's like a sensory deprivation room...

Tim: This is a railway station in Paris

Marie: ...where at first there is nothing and then your imagination takes over

Tim: This is a map of everywhere I've been

Marie: It's a shelter from the elements...

Tim: This is...hard

Marie: It is a deep level particle accelerator

Jake appears SR proscenium arch; Tim carries on with his cards throughout.

Jake: It may seem to you that we've done this for the first time.
Let me refute that here and now. You may think he's wondering whether he has control or not and that the others are disturbing him unnecessarily. Even the mistakes have been repeated over and over to get them exactly right.

Mole enters SLD.

Jake: She looks like she doesn't know what to do next...

Mole takes the cards away from Tim, and gives him a book.

Jake: Of course she knows what she'll do next, it is never different.

Mole removes sheet from Tim's head, whispers in Tim's ear and leaves closing door.

Tim: This is... (confused about what to say about the book in his hands)

Jake: Nothing is left to chance; nothing can go wrong, we've thought of every eventuality.

Marie leaves; Tim is still struggling repeating "This is..."

Jake: It's cast iron, fool proof, unshakeable. If you never believe in anything for the rest of your life believe in this one thing. That absolutely nothing can change the course of what we're doing

Jake turns to leave and bumps in to the set and then leaves.

Tim: This is leaves falling

Marie enters SLD.

Throughout the next sequence, Tim repeats these lines randomly

Tim: This is where I keep my notes
This is where I store my numbers
This is something I take to bed with me
This is the last thing I close at night
This is something I hold under the lamp
This is where I paste my photographs
This helps me to remember

Marie takes the dustsheet off the unoccupied chair and lays it neatly on the table. She takes the book from Tim and lays it on the sheet. Jake enters backwards DSL hatch and walks backwards over his jacket, gets on his knees and holds the edge of his jacket. Marie takes the spare chair to USL corner and sits down. Sarah enters through DSL hatch, closes it and walks backwards on to Jake's jacket. Jake pulls the jacket from under her and she falls to the floor. He puts on his jacket and walks round to the side of Tim's table, with his back to SL wall and puts his hands on opposing corners clutching the sheet. He whips the sheet from the table and the book stays put. Mole enters from SRD, takes the book and quickly exits through door. Tim runs after him. Marie exits SLD. Jake re-covers table with the sheet and sits down. Mole enters SRD and puts a bottle of water on the table and exits (both doors are open). Jake whips sheet away again and bottle stays put.

Jake: Can I have a wine glass please?

Mole appears SRD, puts glass on table and exits. Jake pours some water and drinks it, (Drinking position No 2) and then leaves SRD with sheet.

Mole (SRD) and Marie (SLD) appear with dust-cloths over their heads (the kiss) walk towards each other reach the table and are pulled back by Jake and Tim, this is repeated twice.

All doors and hatches are closed except in the ceiling.

Mole opens SR proscenium arch top hatch with a bottle and Marie opens SL proscenium arch bottom hatch with a glass. After some confusion the hatches are closed.

Simple sums you find a help in times of trouble... even still in the timeless dark you find figures a comfort (Samuel Beckett 1980, p.54-55)

CHAPTER 10

MATHEMATICS

It was necessary to address mathematics in 'Schrödinger's Box' because of its relationship with Quantum Physics. However mathematical models have become practical tools for the company, imposing discipline upon time and space, determining structures and providing consistency.

The basic maths of design, measurement, ratio and geometry are used in the construction of sets, the latter introducing diagonals and establishing perspective and areas of focus, such as in the arrangement of the tables before the drinking scene.

Individual elements can be organised or randomised by allocating numbers and codes i.e. a= apple b = banana c = cat d= density.

'The Last Supper' started out with a clear mathematical structure, with 13 last meal requests, 39 people arranged on 3 tables each seating 13 (and itself an image of 'The Last Supper'). There was originally a set of 52 statements.

The 'Schrödinger's Box' drinking scene is the only scene, apart from the ending, in which all five performers are visible at the same time, and relies upon mathematics for its effect. Four drinking 'actions' each correspond with a number from 1 to 5 (the number '3' doesn't have an action) shouted in sequence by Tim. In between he shouts out the names of objects to be removed from the space. The other performers initially follow his instructions but increasingly go awry with the consequence that the system collapses.

This scene is crucial; not only in the performance but also for me as a maker because with this simple scene of 'shouting' numbers through a hatch I realised that we had previously sat too comfortably within scenarios. We watch as the system that Tim controls disintegrates around him. and without acting 'despair' his repetition of the system leads to a desperately sad situation. Everything he created or controlled falls apart and after some time he is led into the space. still shouting and observing his environment. his system breaks. as he names all the objects in his briefcase.

last meal - Time lapse decomposed

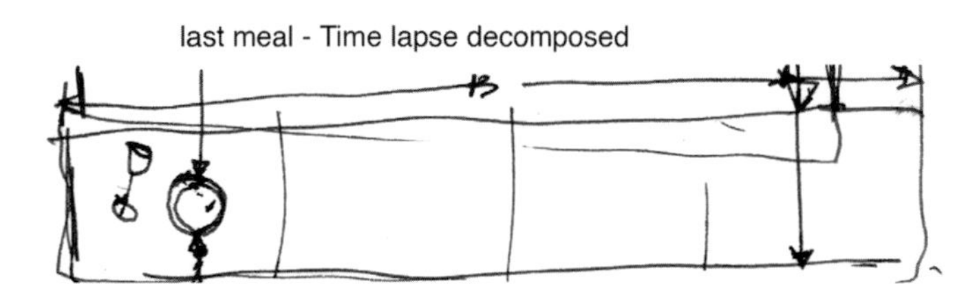

13 Last meal requests.

Shadow of the glass rotates - 24 seconds = 24 hours Sundial
Red wine evaporates.

'Snowstorm' is uttered twice. the second time a ceiling hatch is opened and a torn up letter falls on his head. What Tim creates here is a system of rules. his own world and his desperation comes from trying to maintain a structure that doesn't exist. It's a scene that is both funny and sad at the same time. These funny and sad scenes also exist in 'The Last Supper' (the Hiroshima scene) and the Teddy Bear Picnic dance in 'Spanish Train'

Mathematical formulae are used by Reckless Sleepers as a means of notation i.e. 'A to B, A moves to B, C falls' etc. and playing with formulae even extends to abstract concepts such as

'Schrödinger's Box' = $\frac{\text{Surrealism}}{\text{Quantum Physics}}$

Working with mathematics is particularly useful for workshops because it is a quick and easy way of organising people i.e. numbering movements from 1 to 5, 12 chairs/11 people. In 'Schrödinger's Box' perhaps its biggest contribution has been in the form of 'Contacts', which itself grew out of 'Values'.

Awareness of the codes that operate behind scenes like the drinking scene led to the realisation that with every performance work a different world is created. each with its own language and rules. A different kind of society lives in each of these created environments.

<u>Values</u>

This process was based on the principle that
PEOPLE = OBJECTS = ACTION = PEOPLE
The space has a set value e.g. a value of 4=4 people in the space or 2 people and 2 objects in the space or 1 person doing 1 action and 2 objects. This was developed, using reading, talking, singing as a value and then evolved into:

<u>Contacts</u>

If you sit on a chair that's one contact, the chair and Mole
Touch the table that's 2 contacts
If you lean against the wall that's 3
(The floor doesn't count)
Put the bag on the table, that's now 2
Take the book from the bag; put it on the table, that's now three
That's 4 (having made contact with chair and table, plus the table's contacts with both the bag and book on its surface)
(Tim Ingram's explanation of 'Contacts', October 2006)

Objects used in this process (hammer, book, table, chair, teacup, light, walls, ceiling) are touched or picked up, appearing as though suddenly invested with special powers and are then just as suddenly discarded. Performers forget what they are in contact with, or the implications of touching a table that might have further objects placed upon it. Minds can be observed struggling to respond to change, as the performers find themselves in positions, with combinations of objects and in relation to each other that would never normally occur.

The process probably derived from the performers touching the walls, which were imagined to be magnetised. This touching became a contact, and led onto establishing further contacts within the space. 'Contacts' makes perfect sense when you understand the system, which is why the system is explained beforehand, but in isolation it would be difficult to understand what is taking place. Its rules produce emotional content without the necessity for acting emotional content

It is possible to pit one person whose instruction is to maintain 4 contacts against others, whose task is to either take things away or add to the objects they are in contact with. In Gent, Ine jumped into Tim's arms to add a contact (herself). One person might try to maintain 4 contacts whilst another requires 2, or two people might be trying to keep 4 contacts between them, or any other combination

An unspoken rule is that a contact only counts if you can see it, if it 'exists' i.e. is out of the briefcase. Another is that others can take objects away or move them out of reach, and one has to let it happen. This stylistic device is to be found in much of Reckless Sleepers' work (see 'Passive/Active', page 75) and has its roots in the 'tit for tat' behaviour patterns of Laurel and Hardy.

I think that we did have a conversation. about whether people got it. which is why we have the first counter. Jake counting Tim's contacts. and then I wrote them down and read them aloud.

'Contacts' has moved out of a process into a set of rules. there's a difference. its almost like we are stuck in this world of contacts. I need 4 and he wants 5. this contest is a very human thing and we've reduced it down to mathematics. however we see a struggle. we see an intention. this rule is more than just a game...

Behind 'Contacts' is the notion that odd numbers are good because they produce a tension. Pairs and even numbers make it harder for things to move on. they are balanced and become stuck too readily. With 12 chairs arranged in pairs and 11 people someone is always sat on their own. From this it is possible to construct a simple mathematical structure for movement i.e. any one person cannot sit on their own for more than ten seconds. This corresponds with the number of performers the company uses in its pieces. almost invariably 3 or 5. There is something about the unevenness that makes the whole feel unbalanced. unresolved. and implies that further change can happen.

'Consequences' is another process that uses a simple set of instructions as an improvisational tool. When entering a space your instruction may be 'you are heavy'. 'you fall'. 'you walk backwards' etc. Another person would be given an instruction that is a reaction to this i.e. 'when someone falls you scream'. The instructions are simple but the interpretation becomes far more complex.

What is interesting for me about 'Consequences' is the absence of responsibility. If you respond to the instructions. being from someone else they feel quite liberating.

We use this in 'Breaking Symmetry' and 'Almost Impossible'. Someone else gives us the instructions. or the narrative that we. as artists. interpret in another way.

MATHEMATICS - CONTACTS

11111111111121
111111000011
001100000111
11122211112222
2222333332222
22222222333222
222222233333322
3322211111111
22222222222200
00 NOTHING

Marie opens DSL hatch and gives Sarah, still lying on the floor, a piece of paper.
Sarah gets to her feet. Tim appears SL proscenium arch reading a book, leans on wall.

Sarah: Briefcase

Immediately Mole opens SRD and puts briefcase on table and exits closing door. Jake appears SR proscenium arch wielding hammer. Tim notices him, quickly straightens up and drops the book. Jake quickly leaves.

Sarah: Book

Immediately Marie opens SL proscenium arch bottom hatch and takes the book Tim just dropped. Sarah exits SR door, closing it. As Tim struggles through SL proscenium arch bottom hatch after the book, Marie enters SLD, puts book in briefcase and takes bottle and glass off through door. Mole appears SL proscenium arch to see Tim's feet disappearing through hatch. Tim is then thrown into the interior space from SL door, which is slammed shut and Jake appears at the door's hatch. Sarah opens SR proscenium arch top hatch reading a book, Marie opens SR proscenium arch bottom hatch showing her feet crossed (as if one long person is behind proscenium arch).

Rules
The briefcase is on the table so that = 1 contact and Jake says "1" over and over, Tim touches the chair so that = 2 contacts and Jake repeats "2" and so on while Mole chalks all the numbers on to the proscenium arch.

Action
Tim picks up the briefcase and puts it on the floor, he touches the chair several times to check the rules, he sits down, he pulls the table towards him, he picks up the briefcase with one hand, takes the book out with the other, puts the briefcase down, puts the book on the table, leans on the table, picks up the book, stands up, walks to the edge of the box DSL under hatch 9, leans on the wall reading the book and then quickly straightens and drops the book (Sarah drops her book from SR proscenium arch top hatch at the same time, she and Marie close their hatches together).

Jake: 1 1 1 1 1 1 1 1 1 1 1 1 2 1 1 1 1 1
1 1 0 0 0 0 1 1 0 0 1 1 0 0 0 0 0 1
1 1 1 2 2 2 1 1 2 2 2 2 2 3 3 3 3 3
3 2 2 2 2 2 2 3 2 2 2 2 2 2 2 2 2
2 3 3 3 3 3 3 3 3 3 3 3 2 2 2 2 1 1
1 1 1 1 1 1 1 1 2 2 2 2 2 2 2 2 2 2 0
0 0 nothing.

Jake closes the hatch.
Mole repeats the numbers he has just chalked up and Tim has to make the appropriate contacts with the objects whilst trying to empty the room of furniture through SR door.

Mole: 1 1 1 1 1 1 1 1 1 1 1 1 2 1 1 1 1 1
1 0 0 0 0 1 1 0 0 1 1 0 0 0 0 0 1 1
1 1 2 2 2 1 1 2 2 2 2 2 3 3 3 3 3 3
2 2 2 2 2 2 3 2 2 2 2 2 2 2 2 2 2 2
3 3 3 3 3 3 3 3 3 3 3 2 2 2 2 1 1 1
1 1 1 1 1 1 1 2 2 2 2 2 2 2 2 2 2 0
0 0 nothing.

Tim clears the room except for the corner chair as he is interrupted by Jake entering SL door and leaves it upended on the floor and runs out SR door. Jake lays his jacket quickly on the floor in the centre and rushes out SR door. Sarah calmly enters through SL door and once again stands on Jake's jacket (Mole is still shouting his numbers), Jake enters SL door, closing it, and simulates pulling the jacket from under Sarah by picking her up horizontally.

Tim reaches in and takes jacket

Mole: 2000 nothing.

Jake drops Sarah

1111111111111
121111111000
01100110000
0011112222
11122222222
3333322222
2222223332
2222222233
33332233222
111111112222
2222220000

a b c d e f g h i j k l m n o p q r s t u v w x y z

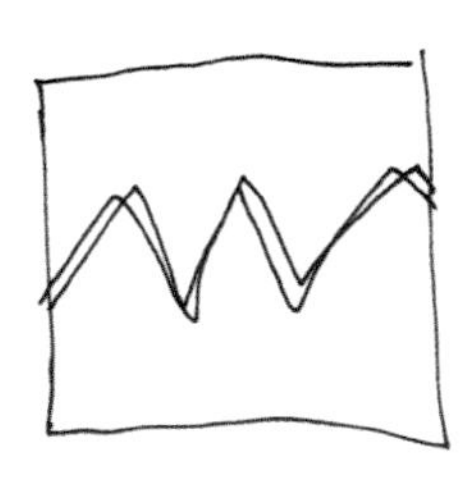

Immediately, the SR door and hatches slam shut.

Jake repositions Sarah DSR under hatch 7 and tries the simulation again. Nothing happens. He turns round to the chair, picks it up and stands it on its feet as he does so Sarah stands up, he turns back to Sarah, is confused and tries the simulation again, this time the SR door opens and he leaves, closing it.

Jake's jacket is thrown through hatch 7, landing on Sarah. She gets up and puts on the jacket, walks to the chair USL corner, moves it to the opposite corner and sits down. Jake opens SR proscenium arch top hatch and we see him in profile, as if Sarah is thinking about him. She sees the chalk marks on the floor, takes off the jacket and cleans the floor. Jake shuts hatch. When she's finished, she throws the jacket through hatch 7 (we the audience don't see him catch it) Sarah waits a moment for it to fall. She leaves through SR door, closing it. Simultaneously, Marie opens DSR hatch, removes the chair and replaces it with an apple, closes hatch.

Mountaineering

Immediately, Jake falls from ceiling hatch 7. Sarah opens the central proscenium hatch (the reckless sleeper) and lies there. Jake crawls to USL wall, makes his way up it as if mountaineering and makes his way around the walls to SRD holding on to door and hatch edges for support. Tim is observing from CSD (centre stage door) SR hatch and making notes.

Sarah: He is forgetful, he is more than just a bit forgetful and because of this he has to be careful, very careful, which is good because it takes his mind off how forgetful he is.
In fact, it takes his mind off what he has forgotten.
He waits sometimes in the gaps between being careful and having forgotten, moving between the two effortlessly enjoying the gaps and enjoying the spaces.
There are things he could do in the gaps, but they pass by him.

If he does remember it is neither a problem nor a hindrance, since he knows he will soon forget again.
Barely noticing anything: the walls and the gaps between them, being careful and having forgotten.

Sarah closes her hatch and Jake opens SR door as he reaches it, exits and closes door. Hatches are closed too.

Outside it might be raining but we never get wet. We talk about outside, even though beyond the space of 'Schrödinger's Box' might not be an exterior space.

We have already suggested that the 'Schrödinger's Box' space is one of many. The ceiling/roof suggests another floor, another level. 'On the roof' can suggest outside.

The outside world is referred to in 'Schrödinger's Box'. 'What is it like outside?'. 'Can you see the mountains?' countered by the answer 'I haven't got that sort of mind'.

CHAPTER 11

INSIDE/OUTSIDE

In most of the places we perform the outside world can be heard, police sirens, shouting and screaming, aeroplanes passing overhead. These noises somehow feel relevant. At one point in a recent performance of 'Spanish Train', a quiet show, I said 'listen' and the noise of an aeroplane could be heard above and inside. I like the idea that we are conscious of this real world. In 'Breaking Symmetry' members of the audience were asked to bring observations from the outside that we performed in the interior space, this interior version of the outside world was played on a TV monitor in the café bar outside the theatre. In the museum project 'Creating the Past' Dan made a soundtrack that included recordings of the ambient sound in the locations where the museum objects were originally found.

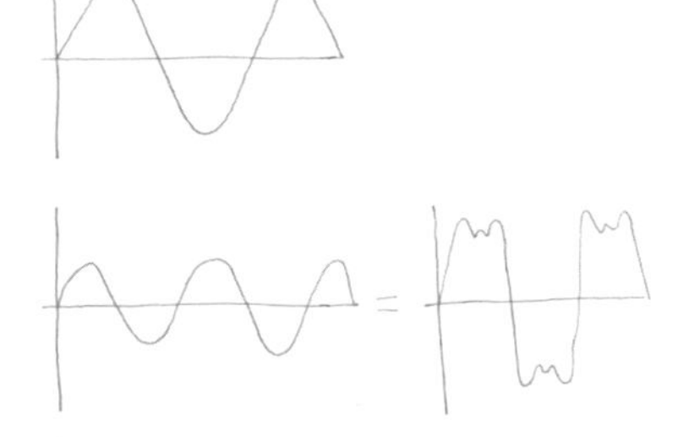

In 'Schrödinger's Box' it rains on the performers, as though their dreams of an outside world have come true. We talk of mountains and reference Heisenberg, the outside world, and the shape of waves like mountains, graphs and interference.

As in lives and conversations around the world, the weather is a central topic. The weather is used by Reckless Sleepers as a means of introducing everyday dialogue. In Gent Leen composed and read a text through one of the small hatches that included long silences and personal asides. A sense of unease was generated by the weathergirl's humanity and vulnerability.

In what was effectively the attic space of Vooruit the wind and rain made it impossible to forget that an outside world existed beyond the studio. In 'Schrödinger's Box' the company plays with the notion of localised weather, rain pouring through a hatch into a briefcase, rain targeting an individual.

In accordance with the rule that materials and objects should exist across a spectrum of states, water should logically appear as not only rain and snow but also steam. The 'Reckless Sleepers' performance in 1988 included a kettle with an element that switched on and off of its own accord. It was not supposed to be in the performance, a cup of tea had simply been requested beforehand and because of its unpredictable nature the kettle was forgotten. People were asking 'how you get it to do that?' The kettle remained in the performance and even reappeared in the next, although its subsequent performances was not felt to be as good.

It is an attempt to tie in 2 different worlds. there's the supposed real world. a conversation about the weather. and then there is the imaginary world of Tim and Fire. The two relate. I don't know why but it seems that these 2 colliding worlds make sense. the weather is referred to later in the weather scene with Leen. it's also trying to work out what is happening outside.

This also refers to wanting to be outside. being trapped and trying to get out. which refers to the cat in the box.

In 'Schrödinger's Box' Jake climbs a mountain scaling the walls of the interior space. The parts that he climbs are the peaks and the troughs of a wave/graph that is drawn towards the end of the piece. He imagines an outside world; he even attempts to climb this mountain. With 'In The Shadow' we describe interior and exterior spaces and often there is a conflict of interest. this culminates with a big shouting scene at the end. This interior/exterior world has often been part of the Reckless Sleepers' repertoire.

In the museum project small houses were placed on a body, as though the body of a landscape. Leen lying on the table, the shape of her body echoed the shape of the wave/mountain chalk drawing on the set.

In 'Spanish Train' it snows. In 'The Last Supper' we describe many exterior spaces. St Helena, on a black rock in the middle of the South Atlantic, oceans, winds, southerly gale force 3. We talk about 'out there', and in the 'Quiet Time' performance we describe in detail the people, places, the streets that surround the venue. In workshops we go for a walk and bring that experience of the outside world to life in the studio. There are many examples of the outside coming inside, although it's rare that we present the inside outside. In the billboard project 'GB Bill' we mostly create landscapes. In 'Shift' we don't make houses or interior spaces. In 'Parasite' we have the outside of the four walls but these come apart behind the audience and the outside becomes the inside.

T Where are you?

S I'm up here.

T Do you need a hand

S Yeah, I'm a bit lost.

T So am I

S Can you see the mountains?

T I don't know, I haven't really got that sort of mind. Ask someone else

S There isn't anyone else.

S. Is that you with the light? PAUSE

Can you just stay still for a minute

MOUNTAIN, MOUNTAIN, MOUNTAIN

Lights out.

The inspection light is turned on back stage and moved.

Tim from back stage:
Where are you?

Sarah from on roof: I'm up here

Tim: Do you need a hand?

Sarah: Yeah, I'm a bit lost

Tim: So am I

Sarah: Can you see the mountains?

Tim: Erm, I don't know, I haven't got that sort of mind. Ask someone else.

Sarah: There isn't anyone else
Is that you with the light?
Can you just stay still for just one minute?

Sarah gets down from the roof at the back.

In the darkness Jake climbs through USL post-box, Mole climbs through DSR post-box. Jake knocks on the CSD SL (centre stage door stage left) hatch, Marie opens it, passes the inspection lamp through to him and watches. Tim watches from SR door hatch, Sarah watches from SL door hatch.

Jake: OK?

Tim/Marie/Sarah: Yes

Jakes takes the inspection lamp and walks towards Mole he takes 2 paces and Marie shouts:

Marie: Stop

Jake walks back to the corner, closes hatch 3 starts again, takes 3 paces towards Mole and Sarah shouts:

Sarah: Stop

Jake stops, closes hatch 5 goes back to the corner and starts again, he reaches Mole and Marie shouts:

Marie/Sarah: Stop

Mole raises his hands to the ceiling as if in surrender and shouts:

Mole: Mountain mountain mountain mountain mountain mountain mountain (continues).

Marie and Sarah enter SL door, they pick Mole up horizontally (like Sarah earlier)
Tim opens DSL hatch, Sarah and Marie push Mole through it (still shouting 'mountain'); he is then thrown out of DSL side door and out into the open. Sarah and Marie follow him through the hatch and Marie drags him around to SL proscenium arch and pushes him up against the wall, she takes a bottle and force-feeds him water in an attempt to stop him from shouting, she backs away and he says

Mole: Mountain mountain mountain

Marie gives him some more from the bottle, moves away, he then whispers

Mole Mountain mountain

Marie gives him some more, this time too much, backs away, Mole stops

There appears to be a connection between Magritte's imagery and the thought experiments used to articulate the concepts behind Quantum Theory i.e. 'this is not a pipe' could equally be 'this is not a dead cat... this cat is alive'. The famous image of the pipe exists alongside text that appears to contradict it. One of them is wrong but neither of them is; they just happen to be together and depend upon one another's existence. In the Quantum realm they are 'superposed'.

CHAPTER 12

MAGRITTE

Magritte is variously referenced in 'Schrödinger's Box'. The 'I am not here', 'this is not a...' motif relates to the initial concept of 'Schrödinger's Box' with 'truth/ non-truth', as well as objects, apples and Surrealism. Magritte is also significant to the company for having painted 'The Reckless Sleeper' ('Le Dormeur Temereire') from which the title of the first performance and the company's name are derived.

In 'Schrödinger's Box' there was deliberate referencing of Magritte's 'The Reckless Sleeper' with Sarah framed in the middle hatch lying on her side whilst other activity was taking place below.

The Lovers - Magritte (1928)

The Treachery of Images - Magritte (1927)

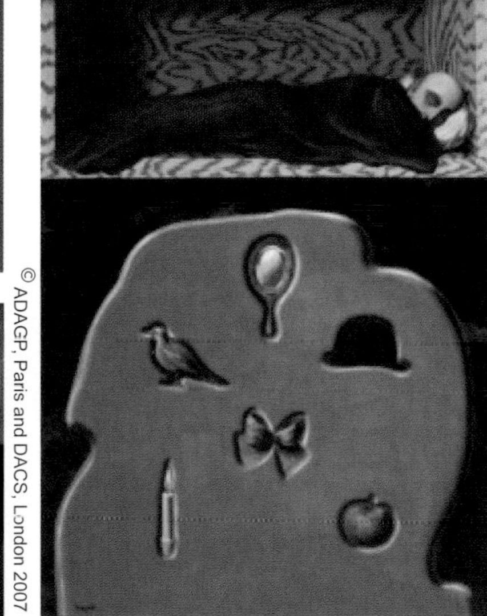

The Reckless Sleeper - Magritte (1928)

A scene in 'Schrödinger's Box' features Mole and Marie with their heads covered by sheets, entering the space from opposing side doors, and moving towards the centre of the space in an attempt to kiss. They are forcefully jerked back from behind on two occasions and fail to make contact, evoking gravitational pull, inevitability, attraction, and repulsion.

In Gent a discussion took place among the artists around the meanings that could be ascribed to the covered heads. Their use by Magritte as a recurring motif in his paintings makes reference to the childhood experience of witnessing his mother pulled from the river in which she had drowned. Her body was naked and her nightgown was obscuring her face. It is hard to escape the connection of the motif with death, execution and ghosts, but to excise a strong image simply because a particular reference could be made seems remiss. Thus there were attempts in Gent to 'reclaim' the image with Tim carrying Leen, both with towels wrapped around their heads.

It is a strong image for me and continues to resonate. with prisoners in Guantanamo Bay. Iraqi prisoners of war. captured hostages. executions. I can't escape it.

Magritte

The company's devising process related to Magritte's paintings involves studying an image and then attempting to articulate it in a physical way, using images to explore alternative actions and scenes. The intention is to communicate a feeling of a picture, not to create a literal description of it. Despite perhaps only producing one moment in a whole week the 'Magritte' process is liberating because images do not have to be produced from scratch. What comes from the process is developed further and does not remain within it.

For 'Schrödinger's Box' Magritte's scenarios offered a snapshot from which there is a before and after, these being moved on 10 seconds or 5 minutes in order to generate movement and ideas.

The 'Magritte' processes are enhanced by the use of imaginary objects, as opposed to real objects. The work of other pre-Surrealist and Surrealist artists can be used for this exercise but whereas Magritte's images are very clear, those of de Chirico contain a different set of meanings. Although the railway references in the latter's work seem interesting they do not lend themselves to this particular process, or this particular piece.

A lead-in process involves the performers observing and then physically placing another person into a particular position. In a related process they watch one of their fellows sitting for 15 minutes and, using pen and paper, describe their movements and attempt to deduce what they are thinking about.

Malo forced Tim into the space with burning objects (although they are not 'seen' until he is upon them). He steps on one small fire, frantically brushing it away, only to find other fires; everywhere he turns new fires seemed to be springing up. We observe him with arms held up across his face, frantically closing hatches.

'First fire'. and the following fires. 'Big fire. 'Fire with another' started with giving Tim an image (Magritte's 'Lechelle') who produced this small section. This for me became a section to develop. and here I see the strength of Tim on stage doing his things. he is very precise about what he shows. In this instance. he also said that he had an image in his head of when we were in the South of France working on 'The Last Supper'. The final week of rehearsal coincided with his birthday and we decided to have a barbecue. which got out of control. I took a photo of Tim behind the flames and he had this image in his head. (I have another image of Laurel and Hardy in 'Swiss Miss')

He was very clear in his mind of an action. this is very much part of the process that we use for making and presenting. For each moment there is a definite idea of the image that we are making. this extends to all performances and all moments.

For 'First fire' and 'Big fire'. I want it also to be repeated. or for Leen to walk into the space and try to see what Tim imagines. When she walks into the space of course there is nothing there. it's obvious that she doesn't see anything. I believe it and push Tim into the space; he doesn't want to go in because he knows that there is something dangerous in there.

A scene that has potential. it also relates to the basic elements. heat. light and energy...

When Tim pretends there is a fire. he is doing something other than stating the obvious; it is neither mime nor acting.

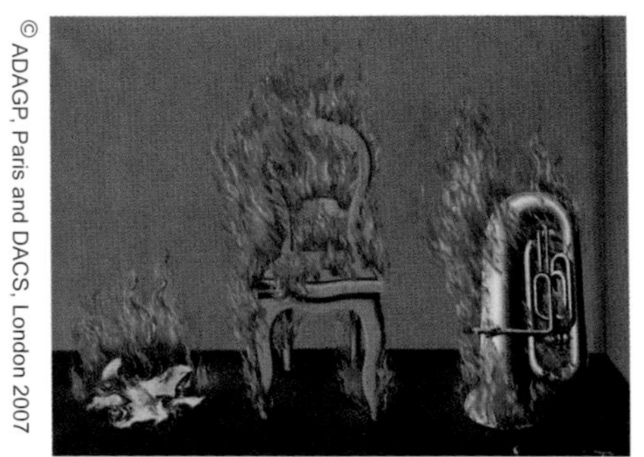

The Fire Ladder - Magritte

3 Magic cups

In '3 Magic cups' one person simply turns away whilst holding a cup to give the illusion of its disappearance while another turns to face the viewer and it reappears. The result is subtle and economical. The person with the cup takes the viewer's attention.

Mole preferred the version in which he drew the cup in white chalk on the black cover of a book. He turned with his back to where the auditorium would be, turned the book so the image was at the front and then turned to face the front, referencing both the magic cups and the objects drawn on the Rorschach cards ('this is...' or 'I see...')

When asked to explain the meanings of the box, Leen seemed to identify with the cat, feeling concerned for it, despite its virtuality. Although the cat and what it is doing has no consequence, one feels an empathy with it in its plight. The box is perceived to be a place of torment and entrapment from which the cat would like to escape.

The cat was felt to be a constant theme. not as a running gag but as though something is missing. like one of us is not here. a performative device. 'That table is not here...' goes back to Magritte's 'this is not a...'

There was a question about the cat not being there. we said that we would use 'Has anyone seen the cat?' It also made sense that if there was a cat there would probably be mice. that we also didn't see. and that lead to mouse traps. and experiments on mice. This is an understanding of the piece that we are experimenting on each other. the scales are different i.e. cat and mouse.

'3 Magic cups' is an example of making something that may not necessarily go into the performance. it's a detail. it's an idea of how to behave. for this particular performance. We started by talking about magic and magicians. or the object in hand being the wrong one for the gesture. For example handing someone a bunch of flowers. but with the wrong object or without an object will have a completely different interpretation. With 'Schrödinger's Box' there are plenty of examples where the object doesn't match the action.

I want someone to hand a watch over. Clocks and time are relevant to this piece. and a broken watch would be a suitable image. relating to the magician's trick of smashing a watch wrapped in a handkerchief. and like the apple that Leen destroys with the hammer.

Another process involved feline behaviour...

I asked that we take traits from cats; in the way they follow light. or shadows. This occupies a cat. especially one confined in a city. as in a more open space they would probably chase leaves or mice. Here we use this as a stimulus. It becomes a detail. it's a behaviour thing. and in no way are we pretending to be cats. Leen comes in to see Tim and can't see what he sees... which also relates to the fire...and we can't see the mountains either. There are plenty of things we can't see. but we imagine them or describe them being there.

List of objects used:

Objects in Reckless Sleepers' work exist as themselves or take the form of words, sounds or drawings, in a similar way to water existing as rain, snow or steam. The letter, when torn up, might represent snow or when read aloud become sound waves. Cards dropped on the floor become stepping-stones.

Reckless Sleepers uses objects that are both archetypal and belonging to the 'everyday'. These objects lend themselves to graphic representation, their use is specific and they are limited in number. Some take a journey from one piece to another; the briefcase and hammer used in 'Schrödinger's Box' also featured in 'Parasite', as did the chairs upon which the audience was seated. The four tables were constructed from the design of the original table in 'Parasite' and 'Push Parallel'.

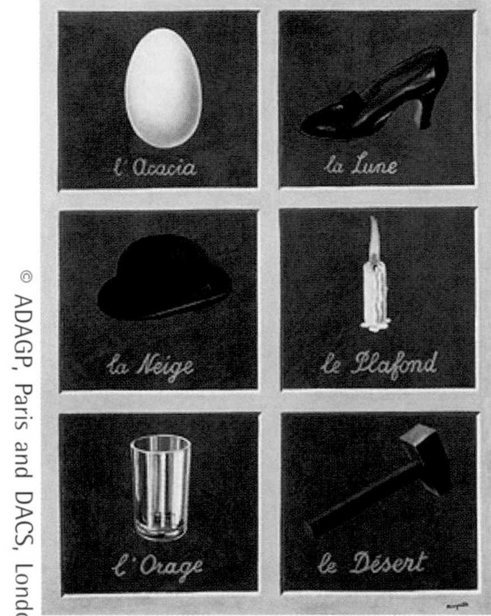

The Key to Dreams - Magritte (1930)

A light bulb. Invented in the 19th century, but a 20th century icon, representing the sun in Picasso's 'Guernica' and an 'idea' in (graphic) cartoons. The bulb's element must be visible. Most contemporary art galleries will probably have an image of one somewhere on display.

I was thinking about objects and their significance, especially in teaching practice. For instance performance studies courses should have in their stores collections of classic objects, like chairs, furniture, a whole wardrobe of contemporary 20th Century clothes. Without these objects it is difficult to see how you can practice contemporary performance.

I was also thinking about Spike Milligan raiding the massive BBC props department, such as for the 'domestic dalek' scene. We paid homage to Spike in 'Terminal', our costumes had labels on, as you would see in Q8. Spike had access to a whole store of objects that he used in the Q series. The costumes still had their labels attached.

Apples appear in most Reckless Sleepers' performances (although 'Spanish Train' featured tomatoes). Apples signify knowledge (in a biblical sense) and Newtonian physics. In 'Schrödinger's Box' Tim creates a tetrahedron using 4 green apples and 6 pencils sharpened at both ends. In 'The Last Supper' apples reference Newton, James Dean (who stopped to buy a bag of apples shortly before his death), Magritte, New York and John Lennon.

Snowstorm appears in 'Terminal' (in reference to 'Citizen Kane'), 'Spanish Train' and 'Schrödinger's Box'.

A saw makes as much sense as a hammer, in terms of the magic 'trick' of sawing a woman in half. It can also be used to make music, to escape the chamber, or to level the legs of the table.

A ladder is a way out or in, functioning as a bridge between worlds. It also has other, practical uses in 'Schrödinger's Box'.

A hammer. Used for making apple mousse, like splitting the atom in a very predetermined way. This action reintegrated the hammer, which was otherwise making only a slight contribution.

A wine glass.

Cup and saucer relates to Meret Oppenheim's fur wrapped objects, which are very 'English' and more of an archetype together than a single cup.

Chair. Great Importance is attached to having the 'right' chair. Classic British stackable school chairs were used in 'Schrödinger's Box' but a thonet (classical bent wood cafe bar chair) refers to a space where drinking takes place.

Plastic flowers or real flowers, to be used in a bunch, ideally the mountain flowers, such as Edelweiss. References love and magic.

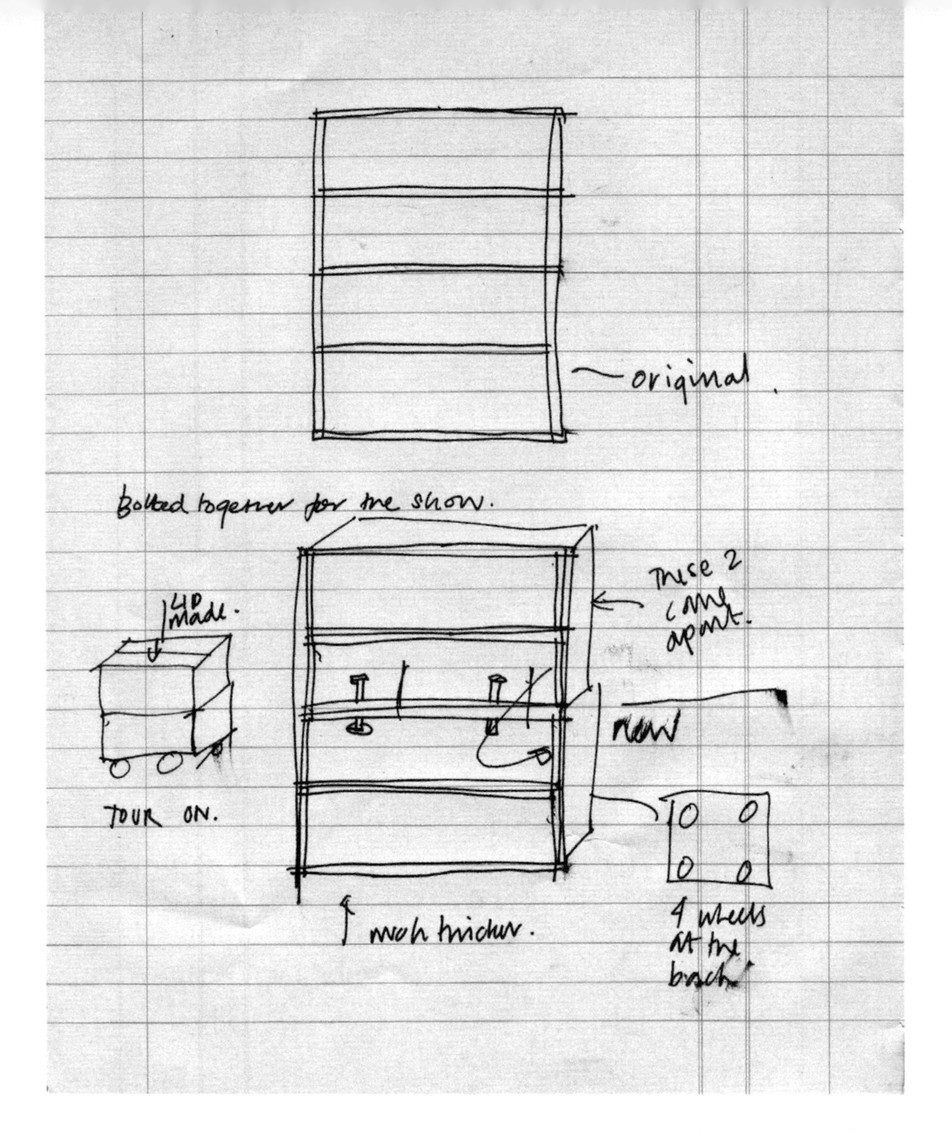

The bookcase functions as more than a possible signifier of (scientific) knowledge.

Although Marcel Duchamp's readymades are inescapable, Magritte and other (pre) Surrealist painters like de Chirico and Delvaux, and Surrealist collage, have heavily influenced the company's use of objects. Fascination with objects is a particularly 20th Century phenomenon and references are ubiquitous i.e. Apple computers, computer icons, signage arrows.

It has multiple uses. originally designed to house a series of box files and all the objects used in the piece. This object goes on tour and so should be economical in terms of space and easy to handle. Ford used to get certain parts delivered by external suppliers in a box that had to fit certain criteria. which was then used in the 'model T' as a trunk or something. A bookcase appears (spoken) in 'In the Shadow'. and its existence leads onto the question. 'which books are in it?' If a shelf. 'which objects are on it?'

I'd like to look at this object as something that can exist in its own right (like Eduardo Paolozzi) and makes me think of 'other' ways of developing things. objects. sculptures from projects. In 'Shift' we contained and supported the books within a series of bookcases. made from Dexion. I think it is possible to continue to make new pieces from these objects. making houses for them.

In Gent various combinations of objects/actions were tried out i.e. light/scream, saw/scream. A performer would be approached by another carrying a light but would be screaming in relation to the saw, image and action juxtaposed and interchangeable until the right combination might occur.

Leen lay on a table, rigid as a piece of wood and the comic effect was explored of Tim screaming at the same time, as she opened her mouth wide. This proved to work best when these were not done together.

Leen and Ine framed parts of themselves, a hand or a stomach visible through the hatches, like an advent calendar filled with body parts.

The mechanics of being in two places at once were explored, a bunch of flowers making an exit by one door and reappearing from a hatch opposite. The action of passing something into the space and a hand going out to receive it was also tried.

'Blindfold' game – A person shouts out a list of objects, two people are wearing blindfolds, one responding to the objects that are natural (e.g. flower) with an action or a movement (e.g. sit on chair or jump up and down) and the other responding to the objects that are man made (e.g. trumpet) with an action or a movement. Whilst this occurs a fourth person writes words on the walls with chalk. This becomes particularly interesting when list of objects became ambiguous e.g. sponge

Each performer could be responsible, or attached to a certain object:
Mole – bottle = (water/alcohol)
Tim – apple = atoms
Leen – scissors = cutting
Ine – chalk = writing

The gesture of a hand opening to accept an object is an example of holding a gesture. like opening both arms to accept a hug. holding the gesture until it is taken. so that it becomes complete when someone else holds that person

I like the idea of producing an object as if from a magician's top hat because it suggests that it comes from the magician's mind. the thought of the object left in his head. as when you think of an object it appears in your head.

The gesture of pulling out a bunch of flowers from a hat is a gesture specific to magicians but like magicians we can pull objects out of the hat (that doesn't exist). whipping out flowers and other things that were previously not there. One could present. with a flourish. the wrong thing (a hammer) then again (a cup and saucer). then again (perhaps a watch that got smashed by the hammer. a magic trick gone wrong) and finally flowers. the right thing so we can move on

I like the idea of smashing a watch. smashing or breaking time. Newtonian Physics describes a 'clockwork' universe. a paradigm broken by Quantum Physics.

In fact everyone has an association with the objects. it is not fixed. But if someone is somehow connected this can produce a sense of tension. For instance if Leen smashes an apple it has consequences for Tim. He can no longer make the atom.

HAMMER BACK LOOK

While this has been going on, Jake moves back upstage centre, still holding the inspection lamp and Tim has rushed on SRD with a table and chair, which he positions centrally, and the briefcase containing a book, which he places to the left of the table, closes door. He now repeats the actions he did for 'Contacts', ending up DSL under hatch 9, leaning against the wall reading a book. While he is doing this, Sarah has reached through CSD SL hatch and replaced Jake's inspection lamp with a hammer and Marie whispers something to Mole and they leave.

Tim looks up from his book, sees Jake with the hammer, quickly straightens up and drops the book. They start 'Contacts' again: Jake rushes at Tim with the hammer, Tim quickly picks up the book and leans against the wall, Jake drops the hammer and snatches the book and throws it DSR, Jake picks up the hammer as Tim rushes DSR picking up the briefcase as he goes and leans against the wall, Jake has to put down the hammer again, Tim moves down SR wall one step at a time to the corner clutching the briefcase followed by Jake. Tim leans against the back wall, Jake kicks the book to his feet (Mole opens DSL hatch and puts a table in the room, closes hatch), Tim drops briefcase comes off the wall and picks up the book, Jake snatches up the hammer and rushes Tim, who quickly sits on the chair and holds the table, Jake has to drop the hammer again.

Tim and Jake stop for a verification of contacts.

Jake picks up the hammer and runs at Tim who quickly gets up with book and throws himself against SLD, Jake leans over him (Marie opens USR hatch and puts a chair in, closes hatch). Tim slides along wall to USL corner, Jake puts hammer on table, Tim steps away from wall, Jake quickly picks up hammer and goes for Tim who slams himself back into corner wall (repeat this two more times). In frustration, Jake throws hammer down, picks up the table and threatens Tim with it, Tim holds the book over his head and threatens Jake with it, who backs away and puts table down under hatch 7 and leans against wall, Tim has to drop the book and Jake picks up the table. Confused, Tim goes upstage and picks up a chair, Jake has to drop the table, Tim drops the chair, Jake picks up table. Repeat for a bit. Mole enters SLD and brings on a table with a bottle of water and a glass and then a chair behind it repeating the same 'Contacts' action of Tim and Jake, leaves closes the door. Jake spots the bottle, stops the game and gestures towards it. They both walk over to the table and stand on either side, Tim with his back to SR wall (Mole opens DSL hatch and puts a chair behind the table, closes hatch), Jake and Tim both go to lean their hands on the table, but realise that it would be too many contacts and pull away quickly at the last moment. Marie comes on SRD and puts a table in front of the chair DSR, she then forcibly grabs Tim and throws him out of the room SRD, she follows him and closes door. In corridor Mole grabs Tim and throws him out USR side door into the open. If there is room Mole will keep hold of Tim and throw him out of the theatre space, Mole leaves him, Tim walks behind set.

CHAPTER 13

ALCOHOL

The company has a complex relationship with alcohol, although work is not usually made directly under the influence. The use of real alcohol would be consistent but in the company's work it relates to the action of drinking, not drunken-ness.

In 'Schrödinger's Box' drinking is used as a means of escape. Marie tries to calm Mole and stop his repeated shouting of 'Mountain' by forcing him to drink. Mole drinks until he physically cannot drink any more. Although it is water, not alcohol, this relates to another rule, that despite being on stage, one does things for real.

Mole's lack of resistance to Marie's action is born of a duality of intention, as really he wants it to happen. This is 'Passive/Active', a company process manifested in various performances.

Tim wrote a piece called 'The Devil' (Duvel) alone in a bar where he was asked to observe and write one evening. This text was condensed into a half hour performance in which he was served by a blindfold waiter (Mole). The number of drinks that he had originally drunk was maintained and he got so drunk it was only performed once.

'Passive/Active' is the name given to a movement process involving two people, one of whom changes the position of the other. It is not a way of generating material, although it is a way of making physical contact with another performer, and finding out what limitations there are.

I let someone do something to me, push my head in a bucket of water, drag me off stage; there is no, or little resistance. And the performer is not always dead, as in 'Spanish Train' when Leen stuffs me, the dead bear, with feathers.

Not quite sure how many people are in here. Thought I was the only one. Please come soon with ~~some~~ Am feeling rather lonely and lost. Need more supplies. don't know

VODKA

In 'Shift' we had one small moment where one of the performers is struck on the head and Dan, who is somewhere else, falls to the floor.

In 'Parasite' Christine MacSween is nailed to the chair, it is an attempt to keep her in a position, she's not dead, just not particularly active.

In 'Push Parallel' I let Debbie, then Julie break a chair to pieces, the one I'm sitting on. I don't stop them. The passive receiver is the focus. It's a great place to be, because the other is busy servicing your pain.

In 'Schrödinger's Box' I am forced to drink water. I know that I can resist it, but there is something stopping me. Tim is blindfolded, but nothing is stopping him taking this off. It is as though these are rules of behaviour and we have to obey them. These rules bind the piece, if we ignored them, or reacted in a normal way i.e. by taking the blindfold off, we wouldn't have a show. This is where the idea of realness is for me, on stage, in a performance breaking down. Perhaps we enjoy being cut, or bashed with a large hammer.

How alcohol is used in 'The Last Supper' is interesting in the way that red wine becomes part of the party that often takes place after the performance, as blood, a social and sharing experience. People are given drinks and become relaxed, thus becoming part of the event, implicated in it.

DRINKING

Jake tentatively picks up the bottle and the glass and walks over to DSR table and places them on it, he then sits down behind the table. Marie and Mole enter SRD, Marie sits at table DSL, Mole sits at table USR. Sarah enters at same time SRD and sits at table USL. They look at Jake's table and suddenly realise they haven't got a bottle and a glass and hurry off to get them through the doors they entered by. They return moments later with bottle and glass and close the doors behind them.

Tim sticks his head through SLD hatch. (There is a rule during this scene that if at any time a glass is broken Tim will shout 'STOP' and everyone will stop at the point they are at. Tim will enter with a dust-pan and brush, clear up the broken glass and then continue where he left off).

Tim shouts 1 and the others react quickly with a drinking action, Tim shouts 2 and the others react quickly with a different drinking action and so on up to 5 (see diagram). This is repeated twice. Tim then shouts Chairs. The chairs are taken out of the space

(Mole throws his and Sarah's chair through USR hatch, Marie takes her and Jake's chairs through DSL hatch, both hatches are then closed). Tim starts again with 1 getting faster and more manic. After a round of this, Tim shouts Tables and the others swap tables (Mole downstage, Jake and Marie upstage, opposite to where they were), Sarah sneaks out through DSL hatch taking the nearest table with her, closing it. Meanwhile, Tim has started another round of 1 2 3 4 5 during which Jake escapes with his table through SRD, closing it. Tim does another round and then he shouts, People. Sarah immediately opens DSL hatch and Mole is sucked backwards towards it and grabbed by Sarah, Jake immediately opens USR hatch and Marie is sucked backwards towards it and grabbed by Jake. Tim shouts from 5 down to 1.

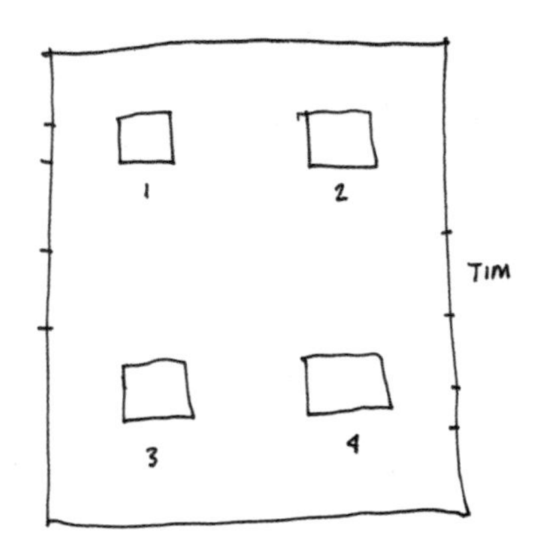

Table positions.

① Left hand up pour drink in glass., lean to the right.

② Right arm, moves glass in an arc towards left hand (whole body turns to L. side)

③ Right hand places glass in Left hand

④ Left hand glass to mouth, and sit up straight, drinking.

⑤ Turn body to face front. left arm moves in arc. placing glass in original position

Stand up: with both hands open in front of R. (glass) L. (bottle).

Stay standing (TOMMY COOPER) glass bottle, bottle glass.

① Sit down,

② Lean R. over to the right side against table surface, so R. arm is flat against it. taking glass in R hand head close to table surface. Bottle in left.

③ Raise elbow L and turn bottle towards glass, pour a drink

④ Drink from the glass, sit up straight slightly.

⑤ Stand up from this position
taking the bottle in Left hand
Sit on the edje of table,
Bring bottle to mouth.
Lean back drinking. · stay in this position until next number is called.

① without chairs repeat this pattern..

④ . kneel on the floor

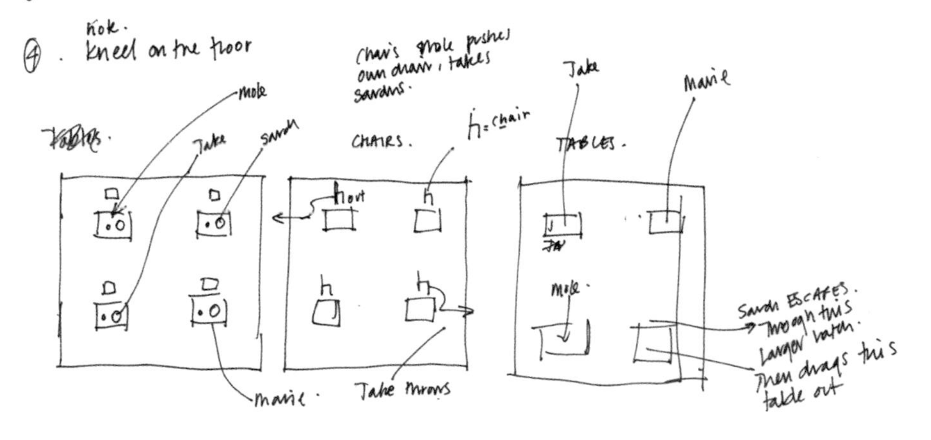

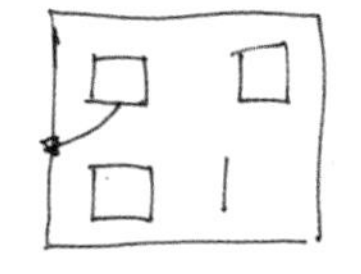

Jake takes this table out of Do.

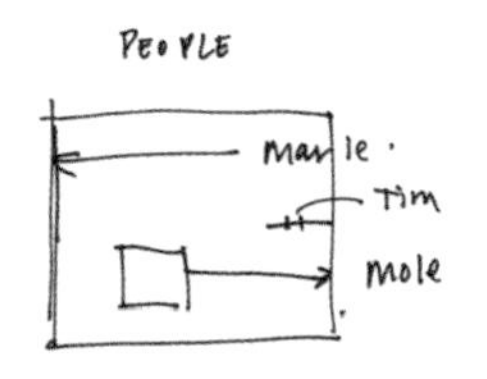

MOLE is THROWN BACK towards the hatch, grabbing Table.
Jake opens hatch: picks up mole through the hatch.
then picks up table

MARIE: Is thrown back towards the hatch, : and tries to get out backwards, Sarah stops her.
She tries forward, is unsucessful,

JAKE: removes the bottle and glass from moles table

TIM: TURNS the DOOR and his attention to the table.

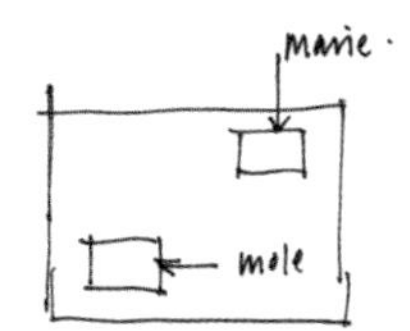

marie fac
mole face

maries table is taken out through this door. by Sarah. (Sarah pushes Marie away)

mole moves this table towards hatch.
Tim can't be seen, so Mole does a version of the instructions. when Tim can be seen again

Mole and Marie try to escape from Sarah and Jake. When Tim calls 1, Jake and Sarah let go. Tim starts 1 2 3 4 5 again. Sarah opens SLD, grabs Marie's table and pulls it out (Tim gets out the way, still shouting numbers), Marie tries to escape through door, but is pushed back in by Sarah and the door is closed. Tim starts 1 2 3 4 5, Mole is the only one responding, Marie moves around the walls of the box from SLD to USR hatch trying to find a way out. Tim starts another round during which he suddenly shouts, People. Jake immediately opens DSL hatch and Mole plus table is sucked towards it, Jake pulls Mole through hatch, Sarah immediately opens USR hatch and Marie, seeing her chance, tries to get through it but Sarah pushes her back in. Tim opens his door 90 degrees so that his head, still through the hatch, is facing the audience and he's shouting at the table. Jake takes the bottle and glass off the table and replaces them with a briefcase, closes hatch. Tim shouting.

Tim: 1, 2 table, 3, briefcase, 4, 5, table briefcase, table briefcase, chair, chair, table briefcase chair, 1, 2, 3 briefcase, 4 table, 5, 1, chair (continues...)

During this, Mole and Jake move to the roof and when Tim shouts 'Chair', Mole drops a chair through hatch 2, closing it. Sarah has thrown Marie back into the room and closed USR hatch, Marie leans exhausted against SRD. Tim carries on yelling at the table. Sarah enters SLD, picks up fallen chair and rights it placing it under hatch 5, she takes Tim by the hand and leads him so he's standing in front of the chair (he's still yelling at the table). Sarah picks up the table and moves it in front of Tim and then pushes him down so he sits on the chair. Immediately Tim shouts Chair and carries on shouting

Chair 1, table 2 briefcase.
Sarah reaches into the briefcase and brings out a snowstorm and places it in Tim's hand. At that moment Tim shouts Snowstorm, which breaks the cycle.

Tim calms down and, apart from the odd word, stops shouting. Sarah exits SLD and closes it and the hatch. Marie has slid down the wall and slumps on the floor. Tim puts down the snowstorm, adjusts his chair and table if necessary and picks up the briefcase. He takes things out of the briefcase and lines them up on the table, introducing them as they appear, thus:

Tim: Apple, apple, apple, apple, apple, pencils (6), pencil sharpener, musical box

Tim puts the briefcase on the floor to his left, picks up the snowstorm and as he shakes it says:

Tim: Snowstorm

Immediately Mole opens hatch 5 and paper snow covers Tim, at the same time hatch 7 opens and Jake falls through. Tim winds up the musical box and puts it on the table. Jake gets himself into a position whereby Marie uses his feet as a bunk up to escape through DSR hatch. Tim locates the book on the floor (still there from 'Hammer Back Look'), and brings it to the table. Sarah appears SR proscenium arch, Mole appears SL proscenium arch with cards, (he shows 4 cards to Sarah and then the audience one by one while Sarah chalks the word MOUNTAIN four times on the arch. Jake starts to do his mountaineering of the set moving down SR wall. Throughout this, Tim is reading his book, making notes in it and eating an apple. After fourth MOUNTAIN Sarah turns to the audience. Marie (from the corridor) follows Jake reaching through the series of hatches marking his climbing points with a chalk mark.

UNTITLED (or trying to explain what has, or is happening)

Sarah: What we cannot see or hear is that there are two others moving around the outside of the box with percussive instruments. The subject in question has to listen carefully to detect the changes in the box. There is some obscure force at work, like the walls are magnetised and he has to cling. This may be because being in the middle is very hazardous or impossible. It is pitch dark to him, but we can see clearly. As he gropes around listening, what he doesn't realise is that the box is being tilted so that the forces keep changing. Interestingly enough, he seems to become quite disorientated.

At this point Jake has made his way around to DSL hatch that is opened by Marie.

Sarah: At one stage in the experiment, he asks for a wine glass to be passed through to him so he can hear the sounds better.
Mole shows Jake an image of a wine glass

Jake reaches the edge of the set DSL and starts retracing his steps, when he has passed DSL hatch, Marie closes it. Mole is still showing the set of cards.

Sarah: What he doesn't realise is that he is not a fellow experimenter but rather he is being experimented upon.
Sarah looks at Mole's cards, chalks up another couple of MOUNTAINs. Marie appears on the roof, makes her way to hatch 2. Sarah and Mole leave. Jake gets under hatch 2 and Marie climbs down through it using Jake as support.
Tim puts apple core in briefcase and starts to make an atom sculpture with apples and pencils (see photo).

Marie leans against SRD again, Jake sneaks out through CSD.

Marie joins up the marks she made earlier to make a mountain range/ graph peaks from CSDL (centre stage door left) along SL wall, out onto SL proscenium arch and down SL side wall,

Sarah chalks up the same along SR external wall, around SR proscenium arch, down SR wall and joins it up to Marie's in the centre.

Tim finishes his atom, puts everything else in the briefcase, clears desk of paper snow and places atom on the table to admire it. Mole opens SL door, Sarah exits, Mole enters, takes atom sculpture and briefcase and leaves closing door.

Mole opens SL proscenium arch bottom hatch, places atom sculpture outside and closes hatch.

Tim quickly clears the paper snowstorm from his table, gets up and chalks an anatomical heart on open hatch 5, he places his chair underneath DSL hatch, positions table underneath hatch 5, opens the centre doors revealing Sarah (SR) and Jake (SL) sat at a table with bottle and glass, chatting quietly with a bookcase behind the table full of box files. Tim moves to DSL hatch, opens it, climbs on chair and through hatch, lifts chair out and closes hatch.

Sarah and Jake chat, Jake drinks, Sarah keeps refilling his glass. What we cannot see is that Marie is stood behind Sarah and she suddenly moves Sarah's chair back so that Sarah disappears off SR. Mole appears from behind Jake and moves the table SR to join Sarah, Mole then moves Jake's chair and Jake forward to meet the table again and so on. This sequence of actions moves Sarah and Jake down the SR corridor, through SRD and into the centre of the room, placing this table in front of the one that's already in there with Sarah SL and Jake SR. Sarah continues to fill Jake's glass as he empties it. As they enter the interior space, Tim appears at SL proscenium arch with box file of papers and starts to read from them addressing Jake and Sarah.

Staring, not talking, not even waiting for their guests anymore
it became a kind of test to validate their friendship and
their place in the world: if they could stay up all night
their friendship would be proved and they would forget
the absence of their friends. They didn't even have any
wine since they were relying on their guests to provide
it. Neither were particularly hungry but.....

Tim: Staring, not talking, not even waiting for their guests anymore it became a kind of test to validate their friendship and their place in the world; if they could stay up all night their friendship would be proved and they would forget the absence of their friends. They didn't even have any wine since they were relying on their guests to provide it. Neither were particularly hungry, but...

Tim throws this text away, tries another one

Tim: The box has the ability to time stretch, time travel, magnify and incorporate the events of a specific place and time.
We are observing its peculiarities and deciding on its function. Don't be afraid to pick up the bottle...

Tim discards this text.

Mole leaves SRD, closing it; Marie leaves SLD, closing it. Tim, frustrated by the wrong text, leaves and walks behind set to SR proscenium arch to try some text there. Mole and Marie go round to the bookcase and get a box file each, Mole then observes from DSR hatch and Marie observes from SLD hatch, both make notes about Jake and Sarah and then about themselves.

Tim: I had to catch my breath, I couldn't breathe without making and shaking a noise that said that I was near, that I was tilted, that my body needed to take in some more oxygen or alcohol I couldn't be sure

Marie then moves to USL hatch to observe, Mole moves to SRD to observe. Jake still drinks. Marie then moves to DSL hatch to observe, Mole moves to USR hatch. Both lean through and chalk notes on wall.

Tim: (Choosing another text). What we cannot see or hear is that there are two others moving around the outside with percussive instruments and the subject in question is having to listen to detect the differences in the chamber. There is an obscure force in the chamber like the walls are magnetised and the subject has to cling to the table. This may be because being in the middle of the chamber is very hazardous or impossible

Mole and Marie start chalking notes on the covers of the box files as well as the walls and hatch doors.

Tim: The air with which we filled our lungs yesterday is becoming unbreathable. The only thing left to do is look straight in front or close our eyes; if we were to turn our heads dizziness would creep straight upon us

Tim closes the box-file, observes the action for a moment and then leaves. Mole and Marie are now frantically scribbling. Tim gets onto the roof and lowers a ladder down through hatch 5 onto the table. Mole and Marie stop chalking, drop the box-files and, without touching the floor, make their way to the table using hatches and chairs as foot and handholds. They then climb the ladder to the roof. Tim gets off roof and makes his way round to SR proscenium arch with a dustsheet and watches action. Sarah gets up and moves round to Jake, who is slumped drunk on the table, and starts force feeding him, first from the glass and then straight from the bottle. Mole lifts ladder back onto roof. With the sheet Tim cleans off the chalk words on proscenium arch, he discovers a book still there from where Sarah dropped it during 'Contacts'. He reads a bit and then starts chalking a diagram and text from the book (see diagram) throughout next scene.

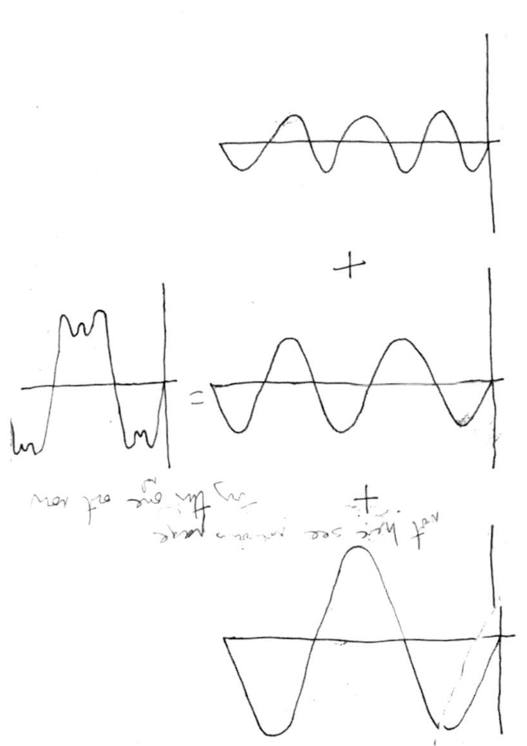

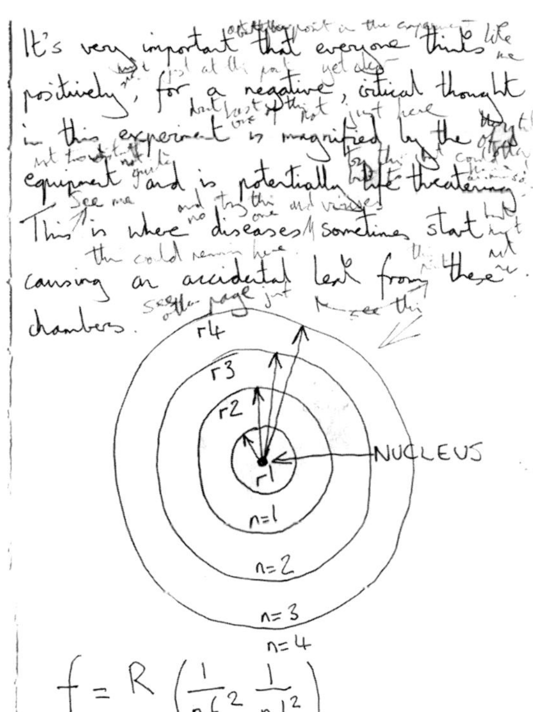

Sarah stops feeding Jake water and removes one of the tables out through CSD. Mole and Marie get down from the roof and in DSL corridor embrace and start rolling along the wall upstage, along backstage wall, down SR corridor wall (both sides), out of SR side door, along SR sidewall, around SR proscenium arch (pushing against Tim) and into the room. During this Jake tries to get up, falls on table and then falls on the floor to his original falling point. Sarah tries to chalk words on him.

Sarah walks out through CSD and starts chalking on the table she removed.

Once in the room, Mole and Marie, still embraced, stand against SRD exhausted, Mole with his back against SRD. Jake tries to get up, but fails and crumples against DSL wall under hatch 9. Marie chalks on the wall next to Mole, Mole turns her so that she is against the wall so he can read what she wrote, Mole now chalks on the wall and so on making their way round the interior of the room until they reach DSL hatch.

During this, Jake manages to get himself through DSL hatch. Sarah then appears at SL proscenium arch top hatch with a bottle, Jake appears at SL proscenium arch bottom hatch with a glass, he climbs halfway out of hatch and reaches his glass up to Sarah who slowly fills it and then Sarah leaves closing hatch. When Mole and Marie reach DSL hatch, Mole throws Marie off him onto DSR wall, Mole takes the glass from Jake and drinks from it.

Marie starts frantically chalking on the wall. Jake gets out of hatch and chalks on proscenium arch. Sarah enters through DSL hatch and starts chalking too.

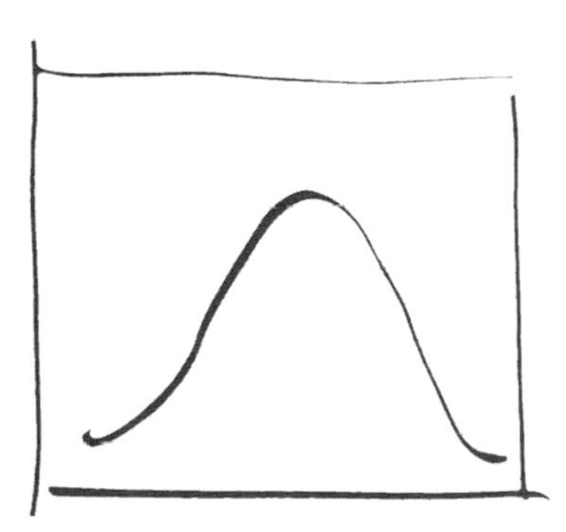

In the closing sequence of 'Schrödinger's Box' it appears to be raining inside the set. The introduction of cold water delivered from above by means of watering cans creates a genuine shock for the performers. They are affected to the extent that it becomes impossible for them to continue and they literally have to catch their breath. This references a line within the letter 'I had to catch my breath, I couldn't breathe...'

The performance/experiment concludes with the performers emerging, all soaked to the skin. They stand, looking back into the box, as if the original scientists surveying their handiwork as if to say 'What have we done?'

CHAPTER 15

ENDINGS

Further development of this ending might play with the conventions of performance by creating a sequence of performances, perhaps over several hours. The 'rain' literally cleanses, wipes the slate clean, ready for the next beginning. As 'Schrödinger's Box' is non linear and has many potential beginnings and endings this device could be used to join consecutive performances.

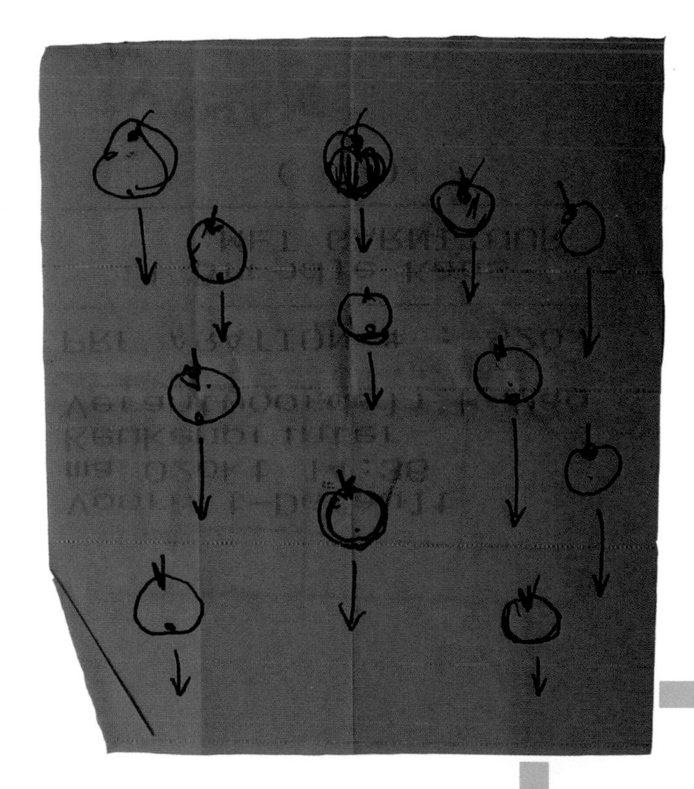

The envisaging of time as a circular phenomenon and a form of entrapment is highly appropriate for the work. A visitor to a gallery when confronted with a video on a loop will tend to stay until the point at which they came in, not necessarily the beginning of the video. While such an idea might be conceptually attractive, it would test the capacities of venues and audiences and place particular stress upon the performers. The conceptual basis might be pushed yet further with progressively older or younger age groups performing it over an extended time frame.

At the end of two weeks in Gent an alternative ending was discussed that involved it raining atom-like apples instead of water, their falling representing the instability of an atomic structure. An unstable element on the periodic table such as Einsteinium (for which the atomic number is 99 with a half life of 472 days) might be used to dictate the number of apples that fall.

The endings of Reckless Sleepers' performances do not take a standard form. In 'Parasite' everything had fallen and Christine was nailed into a chair. The 'Goodnight darling' ending of 'The Last Supper' often breaks down into a social event in which people eat and conversation takes place among the audience and performers. 'Spanish Train' features an ending in which the bear suit previously worn by Mole is turned inside out, releasing a snowstorm of feathers. 'In the Shadow' similarly concluded with a paper snowstorm.

Some experiences continue to resonate, not only in the immediate aftermath of a performance, but in the following days, weeks and years. Waking up the next day or in thirty years time one might have an impression or a need to reconsider what took place. Something of an effective performance remains, informs the way sense is made of the world, and invariably informs further encounters with art.

THE ENDING, OR MEMORIES OF WHAT HAS ALREADY HAPPENED.

The final sequence involves everyone chalking words and pictures from the show on every surface they can, drinking whenever possible, knocking furniture over and throwing water from the bottles over other people's chalked work.

When Tim has finished writing from the book at SR proscenium arch, he goes behind set, gets briefcase and dustsheet, enters the room and tries to sit down with the cloth over his head writing notes on table and briefcase, but things obviously get in the way!

The action builds and builds with people running this way and that, total chaos. Jake ends up on the roof, chalking the outside walls, Mole ends up sat on a chair chalking on the open SRD, Tim is in the middle sat at his table with a sheet over his head, Marie is under open hatch 3 jumping up trying to escape and Sarah is underneath hatch 9 drinking from a bottle.

On the roof Jake has two full watering cans and empties them through the open ceiling hatches on to everyone, starting at hatch 9 and working down to hatch 1. As soon as the water hits the performers they stop their activity.

Jake gets down from the roof and walks round to the front and with his back to the audience, looks in at the chaos they have created. The others join him one by one, they all stand there and look and then slowly disappear around the side of the set.

Music and lights fade, all you can hear is the water dripping.

BIBLIOGRAPHY

- Bannerman, C, Sofaer, J and Watt, J (2006). *Navigating the Unknown: The creative process in contemporary performing arts.* London: Middlesex University Press
- Bannerman, C (2004). *The artist and the process of creation. Reporting on an artist-led study, exploring the dynamic relationship between intuition and craft.* Presented at ESRC seminar 'Creativity, the arts and achievement' at Christchurch University College, England, 5 July 2004. Available at: opencreativity.open.ac.uk/assets/pdf/canterbury/ResCen%20Paper%20for%20CCUC%205%20July.pdf [Accessed July 2006]
- Barrett, W (1990). *Irrational Man.* New York: Random House
- Beckett, S (1980). *Company.* London: Calder
- Calder, J (2001). *The Philosophy of Samuel Beckett.* London: Calder Publications and New Jersey: Riverrun Press
- Childs, N & Walwin, J (eds.) (1998). *A Split Second of Paradise. Live Art and Installation.* London & New York: Rivers Oram Press
- Coleman, J (1963). *Relativity for the Layman.* Harmondsworth: Pelican Books
- Goat Island (2001). *Schoolbook 2.* Chicago: Goat Island
- Hoffmann, B (1968). *The Strange Story of the Quantum.* Harmondsworth: Pelican Books
- Holzhey, M (2005). *Giorgio de Chirico 1888-1978: The Modern Myth.* Köln: Taschen
- Kaye, N (1994). *Postmodernism and Performance.* Basingstoke: The MacMillan Press
- Kirby, M (1987). *A Formalist Theatre.* Philadelphia, University of Pennsylvania Press
- Marshall, I and Zohar, D (1997). *Who's Afraid of Schrodinger's Cat? The New Science Revealed: Quantum Theory, Relativity, Chaos and the New Cosmology.* London: Bloomsbury
- McEvoy, J.P and Zarate. O (1996). *Quantum Theory for Beginners.* Cambridge: Icon Books
- Schechner, R (2003). *Performance Studies, An introduction.* London and New York: Routledge
- Schrödinger, E (1935). Translator: John D. Trimmer (1983). *The Present Situation in Quantum Mechanics* (originally published in Proceedings of the American Philosophical Society, 124, 323-38, and subsequently as Section I.11 of Part I of Quantum Theory and Measurement (J.A. Wheeler and W.H. Zurek, eds., Princeton university Press, New Jersey 1983).) Available at: www.tu-harburg.de/rzt/rzt/it/QM/cat.html [Accessed September 2006]
- Waldberg, P (1965). *Rene Magritte.* Bruxelles: André de Rache

INDEX

TABLE CLOTH:

DRINKING.

JAKE FALLING DOWN:

THOUGHT EXPERIMENT:

VERY VERY SMALL: